EFFECTIVE KEYS TO
SUCCESSFUL
LEADERSHIP

FRANK DAMAZIO

EFFECTIVE KEYS
— TO —

SUCCESSFUL LEADERSHIP

Practical wisdom for senior pastors
appointed by God to lead the local church into its
vision and destiny.

With a Foreword by Pastor Dick Iverson

FRANK DAMAZIO

OnTrack Leadership Institute
領 袖 培 訓 學 院

City Bible Publishing
9200 NE Fremont
Portland, Oregon 97220

Printed in U.S.A.

City Bible Publishing is a ministry of City Bible Church, and is dedicated to
serving the local church and its leaders through the production and distribution
of quality materials.

It is our prayer that these materials, proven in the context of the local church,
will equip leaders in exalting the Lord and extending His kingdom.

*For a free catalog of additional resources from City Bible Publishing please call
1-800-777-6057 or visit our web site at www.citybiblepublishing.com.*

Effective Keys to Successful Leadership
© Copyright 1993 by Frank Damazio
All Rights Reserved

ISBN 0-914936-54-9

ACKNOWLEDGEMENT

To my wife Sharon who has been the co-partner with me in our leadership journey. She has exhibited a Christ-like attitude in all situations, a faith perspective on all ministry decisions, and been a wonderful model of a Christian mother to our four children — Nicole, Bethany, Andrew, and Jessica.

CONTENTS

FOREWORD

The knowledge and suggestions offered here by
Frank Damazio have been proven by years of
experience. Frank and I have worked together for
twenty years. He was in support ministry on my
eldership team, and we remained close while he was
in another city pastoring a church he and his team
started. The practical wisdom he shares, Frank
obtained the old-fashioned way: He took the bumps
and bruises necessary to learn it.

A seniors pastor's job description is complex.
The list of responsibilities would intimidate the faint-
hearted. Unchangeable biblical mandates begin the
list, but farther down the inventory are duties
required because of practical, everyday concerns.
Frank carefully explains the wide variety of pastoral
responsibilities and challenges and shows how many
challenges change with shifts in cultures.

For a church to succeed, the senior pastor and
his eldership must maintain a delicate balance in
government. Extremes produce negative results. A
senior pastor with no checks and balances on his life
can become a dictator and shipwreck the church. On
the other hand, if the eldership rules, the senior man
becomes only a mouthpiece for the elders and
receives direction from them rather than from God.
Men have wrestled with this problem for centuries,
and this book answers many commonly asked
questions.

The pastor, the student aspiring to the ministry, the local church elder, and the person just enjoying church life will be greatly blessed by this look at the ministry through the eyes of a successful pastor. I highly recommend that every leader have this book as a reference in his library.

—Dick Iverson

PREFACE

Dr. Martin Lloyd Jones said a man should enter the Christian ministry only if he cannot stay out of it. I failed to stay out! As I led a team starting a new church, which I pastored the next twelve years, Dr. Jones' warning was etched indelibly into my heart. At the age of thirty, never having been a senior pastor, I had no idea what was in store.

I knew preaching was important and people skills were high on the priority list. However, I really was not prepared to wear the various hats worn by a senior pastor: preacher, counselor, theologian, employer, cultural analyst, decision maker, strategist, administrator, financial planner, and conflict manager. Looking back, I remember the sting of dealing with surprises that come even to successful ministries. I was not aware I needed knowledge of property investment, construction, education of children, fire codes, church bylaws, and constitutions, youth speakers, children's chapels, philosophies of the day, etc.

Bible college had given me excellent training. My experience as an elder in a large, dynamic church, as a Bible college instructor, and as a seminar speaker was enviable. I already had authored a book titled *The Making of a Leader*, however, I found myself not fully prepared for my new venture as the captain of the ship.

I have suffered a few wounds, fallen short of some ministry goals, made a number of poor decisions and had to work through my own wrong attitudes, but by the grace of God, the church lived through it and so did I. In fact, I'm a different man because of it. I have no regrets. If I had it to do all over again, I would make the same choice. This book is a token of what I have learned as the man set in leadership by God to be a senior pastor of a church. Whether you are a senior pastor or are working with one, it is my hope you will be helped and encouraged by this book as you build God's Church.

INTRODUCTION

As a local church adopts a concept of church government, its destiny is being shaped. Church government is the channel through which vision flows. God always selects His leaders carefully, equips them and releases them to accomplish a vision ordained by Him. He gives every local church a destiny to fulfill.

The senior pastor and other leaders implement the vision through teamwork, confirming and releasing ministries. Many times we have witnessed a great vision abandoned because of a division in leadership or a faulty church structure.

. . . .

Let the Lord, the God of the spirits of all flesh, **set a man** over the congregation (Numbers 27:16).

. . . .

The senior pastor is the key leader in God's leadership structure. His office and ministry may be described as general overseer, presiding elder, first among equals, senior pastor, senior minister, or as the Set Man. He is the person in charge, the one with the God-given responsibility to lead and direct the local church. His responsibilities affect every aspect of local church life. If this leader is truly chosen by God to set vision, make decisions (in partnership with elders) and motivate the congregation, and if the leader faithfully seeks God, then the church's destiny will be wonderfully realized.

Then Moses spoke to the Lord, saying: "Let the Lord, the God of the spirits of all flesh, **set a man** over the congregation, who may go out before them and go in before them, who may lead them out and bring them in, that the congregation of the Lord may not be like sheep which have no shepherd." And the Lord said to Moses: "Take Joshua the son of Nun with you, a man in whom is the Spirit, and lay your hand on him; **set him** before Eleazar the priest and before all the congregation, and inaugurate him in their sight. And you shall give some of your authority to him, that all the congregation of the children of Israel may be obedient. He shall stand before Eleazar the priest, who shall inquire before the Lord for him by the judgment of the Urim; at his word they shall go out, and at his word they shall come in, both he and all the children of Israel with him, all the congregation." So Moses did as the Lord commanded him. He took Joshua and **set him** before Eleazar the priest and before all the congregation. And he laid his hands on him and inaugurated him, just as the Lord commanded by the hand of Moses (Numbers 27:15-23).

I will **establish** <u>one shepherd</u> over them, and he shall feed them--My servant David. He shall feed them and be their shepherd (Ezekiel 34:23).

Look also at ships: although they are so large and are driven by fierce winds, they are turned by a very small rudder wherever the **pilot** desires (James 3:4).

Lo, the ships also being of such proportions and driven by hard winds, being steered by the least rudder wherever the impulse of the **helmsman** is intending (Concordant Literal Version).

In this book, the term Set Man is defined as:

A helmsman who stands in his leadership position to direct and manage the church in all areas of spiritual life and vision. He steers the ship according to his God-given gift to lead, his biblical knowledge of the God-given vision and his proven character. He has the ability to raise up leaders and work in a team-like manner in order to equip the church for their God-given task. The Set Man is the senior pastor of the local church, or the key leader in any organization.

This book examines the many-faceted ministry of this crucial position and offers practical wisdom to those desiring to become wise helmsmen steering ships skillfully through calm and stormy seas.

CHAPTER ONE

THE GOVERNMENT OF THE HOUSE

Highlights

- God chooses, calls, and equips leaders for His people.

- Authority structure determines the local church decision-making process, growth limits and leadership philosophy.

- Each local church is accountable for the souls God gives it.

- The local church is a:

  --Dwelling place for God's presence.

  --Vehicle for the moving of God's Holy Spirit.

The form of church government clearly established in Scripture is theocratic in nature. It is not autocratic, governed by one man. It is not bureaucratic, governed by a few. It is not democratic, governed by the people. In a theocracy, God chooses, calls, and equips certain persons to be leaders and rulers for His people. He delegates a measure of authority to them, according to His will. New Testament local church leaders are identified as elders.

Elders are addressed in Scripture as a group, with a plural noun (Titus 1:5; James 5:14). Together, the elders pastor the congregation. The New Testament shows a plural leadership functioning and exercising authority.

In each local eldership, Scripture points to one elder who has the mantle of general overseer or apostolic ministry and who is recognized as the man set in place by God to be the presiding elder or senior pastor of that local church (Acts 14:14, 21-23; 15:6, 22; 21:17-18; 20:28-31). In the New Testament, the church was let by the Apostle James and the elders, Barnabas, Paul and the elders, Timothy and the elders and Peter and the elders.

Note the following Scriptures that refer to elders as the governing body of the local church:

This they also did, and sent it to the **elders** by the hands of Barnabas and Saul (Acts 11:30).

So when they had appointed **elders** in every church, and prayed with fasting, they commended them to the Lord in whom they had believed (Acts 14:23).

And as they went through the cities, they delivered to them the decrees to keep, which were determined by the apostles and **elders** at Jerusalem (Acts 16:4).

The **elders** who are among you I exhort, I who am a **fellow elder** and a witness of the sufferings of Christ, and also a partaker of the glory that will be revealed (I Peter 5:1).

From Miletus he sent to Ephesus and called for the **elders** of the church (Acts 20:17).

Remember **those** who rule over you, who have spoken the word of God to you, whose faith follow, considering the outcome of their conduct (Hebrews 13:7).

Obey **those** who rule over you, and be submissive, for they watch out for your souls, as those who must give account. Let them do so with joy and not with grief, for that would be unprofitable for you (Hebrews 13:17).

(See also Acts 15:4-23; I Timothy 5:17-20; James 5:14; Titus 1:5-11).

The New Testament pattern of theocratic government mirrors the pattern set in the Old Testament. In the Old Testament, the congregation was led by Moses and the elders, Samuel and the elders, Ezra and the elders, Jeremiah and the elders and Joel and the elders. As Moses neared the end of his ministry, he asked the Lord to set a man over the congregation to lead the people as he had done.

> Then Moses spoke to the Lord, saying: "Let the Lord, the God of the spirits of all flesh, **set a man** over the congregation, who may go out before them and go in before them, who may lead them out and bring them in, that the congregation of the Lord may not be like sheep which have no shepherd" (Numbers 27:15-17).

The Lord selected Joshua who was set before Eleazar the priest and the congregation as Moses transferred leadership authority to him.

. . . .

Christ governs through chosen, qualified leaders He has ordained for the task.

. . . .

Every government has a head. Without a head, government does not function well. Headship is the place of authority. Christ is the head of the church. Christ's headship is His authority, His lordship, His rulership, and His kingship (Colossians 1:20-22; Isaiah 9:6-7).

Christ is the head of the local church, yet He governs through His chosen and qualified leaders whom He has ordained for that task.

> And He Himself gave some to be **apostles**, some **prophets**, some **evangelists**, and some **pastors** and **teachers**, for the equipping of the saints for

the work of ministry, for the edifying of the body of Christ (Ephesians 4:11-12).

Let the **elders** who rule well be counted worthy of double honor, especially those who labor in the word and doctrine (I Timothy 5:17).

Theocratic government is God's rule and authority through plural leadership the Bible calls eldership, with a leading elder, senior pastor, or Set Man who is the leader of the leadership team.

Elders must qualify biblically, be knit together in one heart by the Holy Spirit, and understand their role to equip, care for, and protect the flock of God. Eldership will function well when the elders love, honor, and respect the Set Man and one another, allowing unity and strength to permeate the eldership.

The church is a society within a society, a community within a community, a nation within a nation and a divinely governed institution within humanly governed institutions. It is, according to the Scriptures, the vehicle for the kingdom of God.

Every local church has some form of government. The authority in the local church allows leaders to give direction, rule, or management to the affairs of the church. The government of the local church, or the authority structure, will determine the church's decision-making process, growth limits, and leadership philosophy.

It is of utmost importance for church leaders to build with biblical accuracy and godly wisdom. Elders, especially the Set Man, must have a clearly established, biblical understanding of church government, spiritually and practically.

Ephesians 2:20 says the church is "built on the foundation of the apostles and prophets, Jesus Christ Himself being the chief cornerstone." Christ Himself started the church and today he remains busy building it. Twice in the Gospels Christ specifically mentions the church. Once he refers to the mystical, universal church, and once He refers to the local, visible assembly of believers.

About the universal church, Christ said:

And I also say to you that you are Peter, and on this rock I will build My **church,** and the gates of Hades shall not prevail against it. And I will give you the keys of the kingdom of heaven, and whatever you bind on earth will be bound in heaven, and whatever you loose on earth will be loosed in heaven." Then He commanded His disciples that they should tell no one that He was Jesus the Christ (Matthew 16:18-20).

About the local church, Christ said:

But if he will not hear you, take with you one or two more, that 'by the mouth of two or three witnesses every word may be established.' And if he refuses to hear them, tell it to the **church.** But if he refuses even to hear the **church,** let him be to you like a heathen and a tax collector. Assuredly, I say to you, whatever you bind on earth will be bound in heaven, and whatever you loose on earth will be loosed in heaven. Again I say to you that if two of you agree on earth concerning anything that they ask, it will be done for them by My Father in heaven. For where two or three are gathered together in My name, I am there in the midst of them (Matthew 18:16-20).

In the local church, a group of people from a given locality gather to the person of Christ and are marked by a confession of faith, a disciplined lifestyle, and a government of oversight ministries Christ has set in the church. The local church obeys and teaches Christ according to the Great Commission, establishes the first principles of Christ, and keeps the memorial of Christ's death and resurrection in communion.

The local church is a people who come together for a New Testament purpose, who are structured in a New Testament pattern, who live the lifestyle depicted in the New Testament, and who embrace New Testament priorities.

. . . .

It is not enough to belong to the church invisible and mystical.

. . . .

Christ holds each local church responsible for the souls God gives it. The local church is accountable for those souls. In the book of Acts believers were added to the church (2:41). Believers were numbered and accounted for! Acts provides evidence of a visible and practical expression of church membership and identification. It was not enough for believers to belong to the invisible, mystical church, but membership was practically expressed by belonging to the local, visible church (Acts 2:41, 47; Luke 9:1-2; 10:1-2; Acts 1:15).

The Greek word translated church is the word *ecclesia*, which means to call out for the purpose of gathering together as a congregation or an assembly. The *ecclesia* is the called and assembled people of God, called together to listen to or act for God. The local church is a congregation with bishops, deacons, and saints.

> Paul and Timothy, servants of Jesus Christ, to all the **saints** in Christ Jesus who are in Philippi with the **bishops** and **deacons** (Philippians 1:1).

The local church is a dwelling place for God's presence, and a vehicle for the moving of His Holy Spirit.

> Now there are diversities of gifts, but the same Spirit. There are differences of ministries, but the same Lord. And there are diversities of activities, but it is the same God who works all in all. But the manifestation of the Spirit is given to each one for the profit of all: For to one is given the word of wisdom through the Spirit, to another the word of knowledge through the same Spirit, to another faith by the same Spirit, to another gifts of healings by the same Spirit, to another the working of miracles, to another prophecy, to another discerning of spirits, to another different kinds of tongues, to another the interpretation of tongues. But one and the same Spirit works all these things, distributing to each one individually as He wills (I Corinthians 12:4-11).

The local church is the body of Christ where the members join together in family commitment to fulfill their God-given ministries.

> For the equipping of the saints for the work of ministry, for the edifying of the body of Christ, till we all come to the unity of the faith and the knowledge of the Son of God, to a perfect man, to the measure of the stature of the fullness of Christ; that we should no longer be children, tossed to and fro and carried about with every wind of doctrine, by the trickery of men, in the cunning craftiness by which they lie in wait to deceive, but, speaking the truth in love, may grow up in all things into Him who is the head-- Christ--from whom the whole body, joined and knit together by what every joint supplies, according to the effective working by which every part does its share, causes growth of the body for the edifying of itself in love (Ephesians 4:12-16).

. . . .

The local church is a spiritual school where people are equipped and released into their God-given purposes.

. . . .

The local church is an assembly for corporate worship where people gather together to lift up the name of Christ through audible praise and worship (See Hebrews 13:12-15). The local church is a spiritual school where people are equipped and released into their God-given purposes (See Ephesians 4:11-12). The local church is also a spiritual hospital where ministries raise up those who are sick and diseased not only in body, but also in soul and in spirit. The local church is a spiritual deliverance center for P.O.W.s. The power of the Holy Spirit in and through the local church releases and delivers people bound and kept captive by the enemy.

In every city, Christ has one church comprised of many congregations which are part of the whole. The responsibility of each local church is to be under the headship of Christ and to build according to the biblical pattern (See Colossians 1:16-20).

. . . .

Local churches are to be self-supporting, self-governing, and self-propagating.

. . . .

Local churches must recognize each other's sovereignty under Christ's headship and not seek to dominate each other. According to the New Testament no structured denomination headquarters dominates local churches. Each is to be self-supporting, self-governing, and self-propagating.

Local churches should respect one another and flow together in unity, while maintaining their own unique personalities and callings.

The local church has the responsibility to train its own leaders (Ephesians 4:11-14). Each local church also has the responsibility to minister locally to its city and area and to be involved nationally and internationally. The local church is to establish a biblical foundation of

Christ and the apostles upon which to build the house of God with the specific vision given to that local church (See Ephesians 2:10-22).

CHAPTER TWO

GOVERNMENTAL RESPONSIBILITY OF ELDERS

Highlights

- The New Testament lists eldership ministry functions.

- The staff ministries of a church work in partnership with the eldership.

- Elders protect the church from a tyrant ruling pastor who hires, fires, and dominates people.

The New Testament specifically lists several ministry functions of the eldership. Elders govern the local church in all matters of doctrine, morality, church discipline, and financial integrity.

The vision or direction of the church is set by the Set Man or senior pastor of the church. His eldership team does not originate the vision but often shares a partnership with him in setting it.

. . . .

Those who govern the spiritual life of the church should also govern the finances.

. . . .

Usually a successful local church will be established by a leader with one of the five-fold ascension ministry gifts and the gifts of I Corinthians 14, governments, and Romans 12, leadership.

Elders sit on the trustee board which maintains the budget and business aspects of the church. These should be handled by the governmental body of the church, not the deacon/serving body of the church.

Some church governments allow spiritual activities to be taken care of by the eldership, and the practical activities to be taken care of by the deacons or the lay ministries, especially the handling of finances. This structure, can create much tension and misunderstanding in the ministry. Those who govern the spiritual life of the church also should govern the financial life of the church with accountability and credibility.

The annual budget should be confirmed by the entire eldership, but the day-to-day activities can be run by a trustee board made up of elders who can be trusted in the ministry of finance.

The senior pastor should be the presiding elder or chair person at all eldership meetings. The eldership should not convene for business or decision-making meetings without the presence or permission of the senior pastor.

· ·

The wise pastor involves the eldership in the key staffing decisions.

· ·

The staff ministries of a church work in partnership with the entire eldership. Staff ministries are under the direct oversight of the senior pastor. The senior pastor has the authority to hire or release staff ministries in conjunction with the Trustee Board or Board of Directors. Yet, while the senior pastor retains this authority, he is wise to involve the eldership in key staff decisions, to benefit from their wisdom and their knowledge of the people involved.

If the senior pastor releases someone from the staff and also from the eldership, then it becomes an eldership matter. If a staff ministry is released by the senior pastor, and the staff minister feels he has a genuine grievance or has been treated unfairly, he may bring the matter to the eldership. This keeps a check and balance on a potential tyrant ruling pastor who would hire and fire or dominate people without advice from the rest of the eldership.

The eldership should be the final authority in all decisions regarding the purchasing or selling of lands or buildings as well as new building ventures.

The following list includes ministry functions specifically given to elders in Scripture. Also listed are other functions elders perform. These other functions are also found throughout the Bible.

1.   An elder is to be an **overseer**.

    Therefore take heed to yourselves and to all the flock, among which the Holy Spirit has made you overseers, to shepherd the church of God which He purchased with His own blood (Acts 20:28).

    See also I Peter 2:25.

2.   An elder is to be a **ruler**.   The Greek word *proistemi* means to stand before, to preside, practice.

    Let the elders who rule well be counted worthy of double honor, especially those who labor in the word and doctrine (I Timothy 5:17).

    See also Romans 12:8; I Timothy 3:4,5,12; 5:17; I Thessalonians 5:12;

3.   An elder is to be a **feeder**. The Greek word that we translate as shepherd means to tend as a shepherd.

Therefore take heed to yourselves and to all the flock, among which the Holy Spirit has made you overseers, to shepherd the church of God which He purchased with His own blood (Acts 20:28).

See also John 21:15.

4. An elder is to be a **prayer warrior**.

And the prayer of faith will save the sick, and the Lord will raise him up. And if he has committed sins, he will be forgiven. Confess your trespasses to one another, and pray for one another, that you may be healed. The effective, fervent prayer of a righteous man avails much (James 5:15-16).

See also Revelation 5:8; 8:3-4.

5. An elder is to be a **watchman**. The Greek word that we translate as watch means to keep awake.

Blessed are those servants whom the master, when he comes, will find watching. Assuredly, I say to you that he will gird himself and have them sit down to eat, and will come and serve them (Luke 12:37).

See also Acts 20:28-30; I Thessalonians 5:6; Luke 12:39; Ezekiel 33:6-7.

6.   An elder is to be a **student** of the Word.
Be diligent to present yourself approved to God, a worker who does not need to be ashamed, rightly dividing the word of truth (II Timothy 2:15).

See also II Timothy 3:16-17; Titus 3:9.

7.   An elder is to be able to **teach** sound doctrine.

A bishop then must be blameless, the husband of one wife, temperate, sober-minded, of good behavior, hospitable, able to teach...
(I Timothy 3:2).

See also II Timothy 2:24; Titus 1:7.

8.   An elder is to **show compassion.**

I will seek what was lost and bring back what was driven away, bind up the broken and strengthen what was sick; but I will destroy the fat and the strong, and feed them in judgment (Ezekiel 34:16).

See also I Timothy 3:2.

9.   An elder is to be an **example** in all he is, all he says, and all he does. He is to be exemplary in his character, his lifestyle, his family life, his work, and his marriage.

Nor as being lords over those entrusted to you, but being examples to the flock (I Peter 5:3).

See also Philippians 3:17; II Thessalonians 3:9; I Timothy 4:12.

10.   An elder is to be a **leader**.

Remember those who rule over you, who have spoken the word of God to you, whose faith follow, considering the outcome of their conduct (Hebrews 13:7).

See also Hebrews 13:17; Luke 22:26.

11.   An elder is called to **sacrificial service**.

If anyone comes to Me and does not hate his father and mother, wife and children, brothers and sisters, yes, and his own life also, he cannot be My disciple. And whoever does not bear his cross and come after Me cannot be My disciple. For which of you, intending to build a tower, does not sit down first and count the cost, whether he has enough to finish it--lest, after he has laid the foundation, and is not able to finish it, all who see it begin to mock him, saying, "This man began to build and was not able to finish." Or what king, going to make war against another king, does not sit down first and consider whether he is able with ten thousand to meet him who comes against him with twenty thousand? Or else, while the other is still a great way off, he sends a delegation and asks conditions of peace. So likewise, whoever of you does not forsake all that he has cannot be My disciple (Luke 14:25-33).

See also II Samuel 24:24; Romans 12:1-2; Mark 10:42-44.

12.   An elder is to be a **wise counselor.**

For by wise counsel you will wage your own war, and in a multitude of counselors there is safety (Proverbs 24:6).

See also Mark 15:43; Luke 23:50; Psalm 16:7; Proverbs 1:25,30; 20:18; 11:14; 15:22; Isaiah 9:16.

13.   An elder is to **work hard.**

Because for the work of Christ he came close to death, not regarding his life, to supply what was lacking in your service toward me (Philippians 2:30).

See also I Timothy 3:1; I Thessalonians 5:13; I Corinthians 3:13-15; Ephesians 4:12; Proverbs 24:30-34.

14.   An elder is to **bear** burdens.

And let them judge the people at all times. Then it will be that every great matter they shall bring to you, but every small matter they themselves shall judge. So it will be easier for you, for they will bear the burden with you (Exodus 18:22).

See also Deuteronomy 1:12; Numbers 11:11, 17; Galatians 6:5.

15.   An elder is to be a **team man**.

Now he who plants and he who waters are one, and each one will receive his own reward according to his own labor. For we are God's fellow workers; you are God's field, you are God's building (I Corinthians 3:8-9).

See Also Ecclesiastes 4:9-12; Romans 12:3-5; Matthew 18:19-20.

16.   An elder is to **encourage** the brethren.

A word fitly spoken is like apples of gold in settings of silver (Proverbs 25:11).

See also Galatians 6:1-2; Philippians 2:25-27; II Timothy 1:2-4; Philemon 1:10-18; Proverbs 16:24.

17.   An elder is to **share the same vision** as the senior pastor and the other elders and promote unity in the church.

Now I plead with you, brethren, by the name of our Lord Jesus Christ, that you all speak the same thing, and that there be no divisions among you, but that you be perfectly joined together in the same mind and in the same judgment (I Corinthians 1:10).

See also Zechariah 4:1-6; Psalm 133; Ephesians 4:1-3; Isaiah 65:8; Psalm 133:1-2.

18. An elder is to be **transparent**.

Open rebuke is better than love carefully concealed. Faithful are the wounds of a friend, but the kisses of an enemy are deceitful (Proverbs 27:5-6).

19. An elder is to be **submissive**.

The elders who are among you I exhort, I who am a fellow elder and a witness of the sufferings of Christ, and also a partaker of the glory that will be revealed: Shepherd the flock of God which is among you, serving as overseers, not by constraint but willingly, not for dishonest gain but eagerly; Nor as being lords over those entrusted to you, but being examples to the flock (I Peter 5:1-3).

20. An elder is to be a **liberal giver**.

Now concerning the ministering to the saints, it is superfluous for me to write to you; For I know your willingness, about which I boast of you to the Macedonians, that Achaia was ready a year ago; and your zeal has stirred up the majority. Yet I have sent the brethren, lest our boasting of you should be in vain in this respect, that, as I said, you may be ready; Lest if some Macedonians come with me and find you unprepared, we (not to mention you!) should be ashamed of this confident boasting. Therefore I thought it necessary to exhort the brethren to go to you ahead of time, and prepare your bountiful gift beforehand, which you had previously promised, that it may be ready as a matter of generosity and not as a grudging obligation. But this I say: He who sows sparingly will also reap sparingly, and he who sows bountifully will also reap bountifully (II Corinthians 9:1-6).

See also II Corinthians 8:1-15; Malachi 3:4-12.

21.   An elder is to have a **positive** attitude.

Do all things without murmuring and disputing, That you may become blameless and harmless, children of God without fault in the midst of a crooked and perverse generation, among whom you shine as lights in the world (Philippians 2:14-15).

See also John 6:43; Philippians 1:27.

22.   An elder is to lead a **disciplined** lifestyle.

But let each one examine his own work, and then he will have rejoicing in himself alone, and not in another (Galatians 6:4).

See also Proverbs 16:32.

23.   An elder is to be a man of **faith**, one who rises to the challenge.

And David said, "The Lord who delivered me from the paw of the lion and from the paw of the bear, He will deliver me from the hand of this Philistine." And Saul said to David, "Go, and may the Lord be with you" (I Samuel 17:37).

See also Deuteronomy 32:20; Joshua 1:1-16.

24.   An elder is to be a **worshipper**.

The twenty-four elders fall down before Him who sits on the throne and worship Him who lives forever and ever, and cast their crowns before the throne, saying: "You are worthy, O Lord, to receive glory and honor and power; for You created all things, and by Your will they exist and were created" (Revelation 4:10-11).

See also Revelation 4:5-11; 5:1-10

25.   An elder is to **protect** the flock.

Therefore take heed to yourselves and to all the flock, among which the Holy Spirit has made you overseers, to shepherd the church of God which He purchased with His own blood. For I know this, that after my departure savage wolves will come in among you, not sparing the flock. Also from among yourselves men will rise up, speaking perverse things, to draw away the disciples after themselves. Therefore watch, and remember that for three years I did not cease to warn everyone night and day with tears (Acts 20:28-31).

26.   An elder is to be **filled** with the Holy Spirit.

I indeed baptized you with water, but He will baptize you with the Holy Spirit (Mark 1:8).

See also Joel 2:28; Acts 2:4.

27.   An elder is to be **motivated**.

The hand of the diligent will rule, but the slothful will be put to forced labor (Proverbs 12;24).

See also Proverbs 18:9; Philippians 3:13-14.

28.   An elder is to **know** his grace gift and his gift limitations.

For I say, through the grace given to me, to everyone who is among you, not to think of himself more highly than he ought to think, but to think soberly, as God has dealt to each one a measure of faith. For as we have many members in one body, but all the members do not have the same function, So we, being many, are one body in Christ, and individually members of one another. Having then gifts differing according to the grace that is given to us, let us use them: if prophecy, let us prophesy in proportion to our faith; Or ministry, let us use it in our ministering; he who teaches, in teaching; He who exhorts, in exhortation; he who gives, with liberality; he who leads, with diligence; he who shows mercy, with cheerfulness (Romans 12:3-9).

See also I Corinthians 12:28; Ephesians 4:7-11; I Peter 4:10; I Timothy 4:14-15; II Timothy 1:6-7.

29.   An elder should **listen** to constructive criticism.

Listen to counsel and receive instruction, that you may be wise in your latter days (Proverbs 19:20).

See also Proverbs 19:20.

30.   An elder is to **practice** loyalty.

A friend loves at all times, and a brother is born for adversity (Proverbs 17:17).

For the character qualifications of an elder, refer to my book, *The Making of a Leader*.[1]

CHAPTER THREE

THE LEADERSHIP TEAM AND THE SET MAN

Highlights

- All ministries have value.

- One-man ministry is limited.

- Bearing the burden alone exacts a price.

- Convictions support creativity and faithfulness.

- Setting and executing team goals.

- Give-it-all attitude motivates team members.

- Set Man equips and develops leaders.

The team concept or support-ministry principle has been proven throughout Scripture and history to be one of the most effective dynamics of any healthy, successful local church. As we build strong, long-lasting churches, we want to learn from the mistakes of previous generations. One mistake made repeatedly is the suppression of the laity and the exaltation of the clergy. We want to give proper scriptural value to all ministries in the church, not just to the senior pastor. Joseph never was the senior leader of Egypt, yet he saved two entire nations!

Team Definition
When leadership ministries are harnessed together by the Holy Spirit to work in cooperation, their effectiveness is multiplied. Recognizing and submitting to each other, they work toward a common goal, and truly become a leadership team.

> Two are better than one, because they have a good reward for their labor. For if they fall, one will lift up his companion. But woe to him who is alone when he falls, for he has no one to help him up. Again, if two lie down together, they will keep warm; but how can one be warm alone? Though one may be overpowered by another, two can withstand him. and a threefold cord is not quickly broken (Ecclesiastes 4:9-12).

> Can two walk together, unless they are agreed? (Amos 3:3).

See also Matthew 11:29-30; Proverbs 11:14; 15:22; 24:6; Psalm 133.

Down at Fisherman's Wharf in San Francisco we once saw a real one-man band. He was an energetic man playing several instruments at one time, using both his feet, his hands, and his mouth. He was quite amusing--an amazingly creative, talented crowd pleaser. But he was a freak, a unique sort of human show. He was not the norm!

So we have the spiritual parallel in the modern day pastor. Howard Snyder in his book, *The Problem of Wine Skins,* has a chapter entitled "Must the Pastor be a Super Star?" He says,

Meet Pastor Jones, superstar. He can preach, counsel, evangelize, administrate, conciliate, communicate, and sometimes even integrate. He can also raise the budget. He handles Sunday morning better than any quiz master on weekday television. He is better with words than most political candidates. As a scholar, he surpasses many seminary professors. No church social function would be complete without him. [2]

. . . .

A one-man operation destroys leadership in others.

. . . .

One man is limited in his leadership style and effectiveness. One man may fail at wisdom and judgment at times. One man is limited in gifts and ministries to minister to the whole body of Christ. Even if the man is an apostle of apostles, still he is only one-fifth of the five ascension gift ministries. One man cannot shepherd the flock of God biblically. He may burn out, suffer mentally, or crash morally. One man cannot possibly meet the needs of everyone. That is why the Set Man must raise up a leadership team and not try to be a one-man band.

Ministering alone, one man has no one to correct, adjust, or change his decisions or doctrine. He may become a pastor potentate, seeing himself as always right and never wanting to change any of his ideas. A team brings reality to the Set Man and to the church. A team may raise questions and bring up other aspects of a doctrine or idea.

One man may have a difficult time in successfully hearing God for major directions or transitions in the church. Although we believe the Set Man is a person who should hear from God and give overall direction to the church, there are critical times in buying property, building programs, sending out ministries, choosing staff, letting staff go, or disciplining someone in the church where you need more than one opinion. You need the whole leadership to cooperate together to hear from God in unison.

One man cannot carry the burden alone without paying a price physically, emotionally, and spiritually.

> So Moses' father-in-law said to him, "The thing that you do is not good. Both you and these people who are with **you will surely wear yourselves out.** For this thing is too much for you; you are not able to perform it by yourself" (Exodus 18:17-18).

A one-man operation destroys leadership in others, stifles creativity, and runs the risk of producing spiritual robots and ministry puppets.

. . . .

It is impossible for one person to meet the need of an entire flock!

. . . .

The cultural model of the senior pastor being the only person to do the work of pastoring or other forms of ministry produces weak churches, which do not grow. No one, single pastor is equipped to meet the needs of the entire flock. It is obviously impossible, yet many churches still operate as if the ministry resides in one person.

Bill Hull addresses this problem in his book *Disciple Making Pastor*. He says,

> The pastor of the church is the combined gifts, wisdom, and faith of a pastoral team, namely the elders. In most churches a full-time paid pastor and several ministers known as laymen would compose this group. Larger churches would combine several full-time staff with the ministers to form a pastoral team. The plural use of pastor/teacher indicated several leaders per local church, engaged in pastoring the flock. This does not preclude the role of professional clergy. In fact it enlarges their importance and removes a great deal of triviality from their lives. The emphasis on plurality of authority and giftedness on one hand and the necessity of strong leadership from one person on the other, appears contradictory. The dual emphasis is no

contradiction, but rather a call to balance. The balance of a group of gifted leaders called to pastor the church and the leader of gifted leaders to set the pace. [3]

Let us consider the function of the team of workers who work with the Set Man to fulfill vision and destiny.

Support Ministry Definition

A support minister is a person who functions in a leadership role as an elder, deacon, staff ministry, department head, or care leader, fulfilling the ministry Christ has given him in the local church in support of the senior pastor or Set Man.

· ·

A servant becomes great by making others successful.

· ·

All those who function on the team are to be called by the Lord and equipped with the doctrine, philosophy, and vision of that house. The team members should have convictions which allow them to function faithfully and yet creatively. The biblical pattern of the New Testament local church requires the symphonic blending of many different ministries.

Team members should have:

•	A conviction that God has placed them where they are for His pleasure and His purpose, and for their good.

• A conviction that places Christ and His people above all of the leaders' own desires, ambitions, and opinions. Team members must see the ministry as a way to serve and to give rather than as a way to fulfill or promote themselves.

• A willingness to accept any assignment necessary to advance the team's overall vision. A team member must reject position-consciousness, or an others-should-thank-me, recognize-me, or reward-me attitude. A servant becomes great by making others successful. Therefore, a team member must come with a servant's

. . . .

A servant serves for the good of the overall vision.

. . . .

spirit and a servant's heart, having the overall vision of the church in mind. He can never just serve in the areas that he likes, or the areas that he thinks will be the most fruitful and the most satisfying. He serves for the good of the whole body and the overall vision.

• A conviction of loyalty that will save the church and the team in a time of testing. This conviction can only be proven when there is disagreement, disappointment, or disillusionment. This conviction keeps the larger picture in mind. Loyalty handles complaints and criticisms easily because it understands the sad results of disunity and discord. Loyalty refuses to deny its commitment to others regardless of the cost. The loyal servant stands with those he is serving in their time of need. Loyalty and servanthood make great team members. Those who have these convictions always seem to have a lot of responsibility and are involved in every key area of the church. Remember the adage, "The hair on the back of a good donkey is always worn thin."

• A conviction of faithfulness. The faithful team member understands promotion comes from the Lord, and the Lord promotes based on His principles. The principles of faithfulness and integrity are basic to leadership. To be faithful in that which is least, qualifies a person to receive more. The reward of a job done well is another job.

. . . .

Availability is usually more important than capacity.

. . . .

• A conviction of availability. Team members see availability as the needed ingredient to being a useful vessel to God, to other leaders, and to those being served. Being available requires good discipline of time and priorities. Availability is usually much more important than capacity.

SEVEN ESSENTIALS OF A WINNING TEAM

1. A winning leader.

A winning leader has the ability to clearly communicate a vision that excites the team to action. He understands the source and proper use of power and authority. The winning leader desires to respond to the needs of others. He is a people person.

. . . .

The winning leader has a high tolerance for experimentation.

. . . .

As the team catches a spirit of faith, excitement and enthusiasm will result. This will set in motion team members who will stretch out to become excellent. This, of course necessitates experimentation. The winning leader has a high tolerance for experimentation and failure. He never condemns innovation even if it doesn't always produce the right results.

TEAMWORK:
A Lesson Without Words

2.   Tangible goals.

The Greek word for bishop is the word *episkopos,* an overseer.   The word *skopos* means to see or the ability to fix your eye on a certain mark.   The very word used in the New Testament for the leadership of the church has to do with perception, focus, vision.   A winning team must have a vision, a mark to hit with tangible goals.   The team must know where it is going and how it is going to get there.

3.   A "give-it-all-it-takes" attitude.

To create this kind of an attitude there must be a clear vision and clear articulate goals.   Vision causes a person to put the needs of the group before their own needs.   The word here is sacrifice.   A give-it-all-it-takes attitude is contagious.   This attitude will motivate the team beyond the human level of achievement.

4.   The ability to recover from failures.

Don't make a big deal out of your personal failures, failures of those on the team, or team failures. One of the worst traps to fall into as a team is to allow criticism or blame to fall when things go worse than expected.   Examine each mistake and the results honestly, but avoid blaming others.   Analyze how and why the failure occurred, learn from it, encourage one another, and go on.   Concentrate on the lessons learned, not on failures.

5.   **Respect for the value of each person as well as for others' talents and gifts.**

Everyone needs to feel love and acceptance, especially from those they love and respect. Peer level respect is worth more than silver or gold. Each team member must verbalize his love and respect to the other team members. Habitual, continual, and sincere appreciation goes a long way in producing team spirit. Get into the habit of dropping one another little notes, cards, and letters. Make that phone call!

6.   **Intensity and excellence.**

A winning team must never allow victory to take the edge off spiritual hunger or alertness.

Napoleon has well said, "The most dangerous moment comes with victory." The moment we reach those long awaited goals or accomplish the most impossible task, we are in spiritual danger. A mature team keeps the tension of prayer, the need for God, and humility after great victories.

7.   **Adherence to basic principles.**

The principle of reviewing the basics has won many games in sports. Great coaches have built this into their teams. Why? So that in a time of crisis, breaking point, or emotional tension the team will function out of principle rather than talent.

. . . .

Always extend the leadership base
before adding more ministries.

. . . .

The charismatic or gifted player may play well
when he's hot, but what about those slump times? It is
unusual for the whole team to be in a slump if they are
playing team ball and obeying basic principles.

The basics for the leadership team in a local
church are prayer, Word of God, integrity, unity,
respect, love, forgiveness, preferring one another,
sacrifice, etc.

The ministry God has given the church expands
as leaders develop. As the church grows, we need
multiplication on all leadership levels. The larger the
church grows, the wider the leadership base must be
developed. Always extend the leadership base before
adding more ministries. When this happens we can
avoid placing incompetent or unqualified persons in
particular positions. The main focus of the Set Man
should be to equip current leaders and to develop
future leaders.

Here are priority codes for spending time with
different kinds of people:

V.I.P
Very Important People
(Your current leaders)

V.T.P.
Very Teachable People
(Your potential future leaders)

V.N.P.
Very Nice People
(Your encouraging sheep)

V.D.P.
Very Draining People
(You-never-solve-their-problem people)

With whom are you spending most of your time?

GEESE FLYING IN"V"

TEAM WISDOM FROM NATURE

When you see geese heading south for the winter, notice their "V" formation. Scientists have discovered that as each bird flaps its wings, it creates an uplift for the bird immediately following. By flying in a V formation, the whole flock adds at least 70 percent greater flying range than if each bird flew on its own. We can learn some basic truths from the geese.

. . . .

If we have as much sense as a goose, we will stay in formation with those who are headed in the same direction.

. . . .

First of all, people who share a common direction and sense of community can get where they are going more quickly and easily because they travel on the thrust of one another.

Second, whenever a goose falls out of formation, it suddenly feels the drag and resistance of trying to go it alone and quickly gets back into formation to take advantage of the lifting power of the bird immediately in front. If we have as much sense as a goose, we will stay in formation with those who are headed the same way we are.

Third, when the lead goose gets tired, he moves back in the formation and another goose flies point. It pays to take turns doing hard jobs.

Fourth, the geese flying in the back of the formation honk to encourage those up front to keep up the speed. We need to be careful what we say when we honk from behind.

Finally, when a goose gets sick or is wounded by gunshot and falls out, two geese fall out of formation and follow him down to help and protect him. They stay with him until he is either able to fly, or until he is dead. Then they launch out on their own or with another formation to catch up with their group. In the same way, we should stand by each other, protect one another and make new friends with those who seem to be going our direction.

CHAPTER FOUR

COMMON PROBLEMS IN LEADERSHIP

Highlights

- Never compromise major doctrines

- Disloyalty is dangerous.

- Never devour another leader.

- The problem of being position-minded.

- Keep a sober estimation of your own ministry.

- Time limits relationship-building.

- Leaders agree on basic standards.

Several common problems and pitfalls show up in all churches. Leadership teams can expect to have to deal with the following problems:

• **The problem of doctrinal incompatibility.**

Doctrinal incompatibility should be discussed openly as leaders are trained to be vital influences in the local church.

Major doctrines established by biblical mandate should never be compromised. These include the deity of Christ, the atonement, justification, salvation, baptism in water by immersion, baptism of the Holy Spirit, and the bodily second coming of Christ.

Other doctrines without clear biblical mandates may vary from church to church but every leadership team has to unite behind the set of doctrines taught in its own local assembly. Doctrinal incompatibility in the area of church government, for instance, becomes an irritation in the leadership and will cause division sooner or later. Teaching on controversial subjects such as inner healing, Christian psychology, demonology, Christian involvement in politics, divorce, as well as divorce and remarriage, needs to be clarified to avoid needless divisions.

• **The problem of disloyalty in attitude or action.**

Disloyalty does not develop suddenly one day or grow quickly in just a month. It usually begins with an unresolved offense or a philosophical difference which has not been handled properly, causing someone to become offended. Out of this arises a spirit of criticism and ultimately disloyalty.

· ·

Disloyalty is an attitude of the spirit.

· ·

Disloyalty is one of the most dangerous sins in leadership and one that can devastate the church the most. Disloyalty is not just an attitude of the mind, it is an attitude of the spirit and will spread throughout the congregation if not checked. All leadership teams can benefit from reading *The Tale of Three Kings* by Gene Edwards. [4]

• **The problem of philosophical differences that divide.**

Most churches are not in division because of doctrinal incompatibility. Most eldership or leadership problems arise out of a philosophical difference.

· ·

Most leadership problems stem from philosophical differences.

· ·

We all believe in worship. But what is our philosophy concerning the mood of the church service? What are our feelings on drums, guitars, pipe organ, standing, and sitting? Do we sing too many hymns, not enough hymns, too many choruses, too many long choruses, not enough Jesus choruses, to many short choruses? Now we have questions of differing taste philosophy.

What is the team's philosophy concerning women's ministry, evangelism, finances, and decision making? Where a difference of philosophy exits there soon will be a difference of spirit, which ultimately will divide the eldership.

- **The problem of prejudging actions by questioning motives.**

If we get into the habit of judging others by our own level of discernment, questioning their motives and actions, it will cause many problems in the leadership team. We must be, according to I Corinthians 13, ones who see and believe all things are good. We must see good in one another and believe others have good motives. We see people through our own eyes and question them because we ourselves have a problem.

- **The problem of allowing disciples to praise some and devour others.**

Some people in the church will become a disciple of one elder or leader and may see the leader's ministry as the greatest and most important ministry in the church. That disciple might praise the leader's ministry by comparing it with another one in the church, tearing down the other ministry.

Leaders can never allow anyone to devour another leader for any reason--especially by comparison. Team members should stop the conversation immediately and not allow people to pull down any leader's reputation or ministry through criticism.

• **The problem of becoming position-minded.**

Let's be honest. Whenever a person takes a position, he receives certain privileges, honors, and respect from the people.

. . . .

A position-minded leader will not serve his way into the ministry.

. . . .

A person concerned about his prestige can be very shrewd and manipulative trying to gain a position. His motive is not to serve the people but to get the people to serve him and his position, to get honor from them instead of giving them the honor they need.

A position-minded leader usually will not become involved with the menial tasks of the local church. He will not serve his way into the ministry. He will only choose leadership tasks which bring him to the limelight. This person can be dangerous because he may often consciously or unconsciously use some form of deception or manipulation to possess a position. If a position is not handed to him, he may turn on both the church and the leadership and devour them. He then may make the church appear to be at fault, when in fact the position-minded spirit of the individual caused the trouble. Many deal with this problem their entire lives.

- **The problem of those who overestimate their own abilities and ministry.**

It is God who recognizes, promotes, and places people in the right places and positions in the local church. If the leadership and others around do not perceive a particular gift in a person, there is a strong possibility it is not resident. We need to be very careful

. . . .

If we overestimate our ministry, we will become frustrated when others don't see it.

. . . .

to have a sober estimation of our own ministry (See Romans 12:1-3).

If we have an overestimation of our ministry we will become frustrated when others don't see it as we do. We will become critical and ultimately bitter toward those who are over us because they did not recognize our ministry.

Occasionally a wife tells her husband she sees him in a certain ministry. She praises him and lifts him up, pushing him into a ministry which God may not have given him. This is a very sensitive situation. How can you correct a man's wife without offending the man? It is almost impossible!

If the wife has a vision for the husband that the husband does not have for himself, it eventually will create great problems in his home and in the church.

• The problem of unmet expectations in relationships which turn to disappointment and criticism.

Normally in the church we use terms like family, covenant commitment, covenant relationship, etc. We use many terms which speak of our desire to be close to one another and support one another. Those desires are honest and sincere. We all want to support and encourage those we work with and those in the body of Christ. Sometimes in order to be an encourager and a supporter we spread ourselves too thin and are not able to develop deep relationships with many people. This may become a point of contention.

. . . .

We will not be best friends with everyone in our church.

. . . .

The senior pastor continually deals with people who want to be close. There is not always time, however, to develop that kind of a covenantal relationship. This may eventually cause offense, if it is not handled openly and honestly with the wisdom of the Holy Spirit.

We all have a covenant in Christ. We all are brothers and sisters in Christ and are part of the whole family of God. We all are called to koinonia, the kind of fellowship practiced by the church in the book of Acts. We will not all, however, be best friends with everyone in our local church. Most relational research has discovered a person can only have three or four very close friends which they spend a lot of time with--maybe only one or two.

As a leadership team grows, people will naturally be drawn together into close relationships. This is not a problem for the senior pastor or for the leaders. Let people grow together naturally and spiritually. Do not try to make everyone your Jonathan or your Peter, James and John.

- **The problem of ignoring basic standards or basic philosophies already established or agreed upon.**

As the church becomes established and the leadership team begins to grow, certain basic philosophies, doctrines, and vision values will be adopted within that team to lead the church. Once these are agreed upon, articulated, and established in the local church, it is negative to try to change or ignore them, unless they are changed or ignored within the leadership team itself.

Problems will arise if a few leaders choose to ignore basic standards clearly established. An established basic standard needs to be respected and honored by the leadership. Things such as giving, praying, worshipping, witnessing, holiness, love and reaching out to people are basic standards for the local church. As standard bearers, leaders should lift up the basic values of the church.

I ask my leadership team to honor the following twelve basic standards:

1. Be on time for appointments.
2. Be on time for prayer before service or at prayer meetings.

3.   Be on time for leadership activities.
4.   Be a participator in worship, not a spectator.
5.   Be involved with as many weddings and funerals as possible.
6.   Be faithful to attend public worship services.
7.   Be conscientious of all reports and paperwork due.
8.   Be fervent and enthusiastic in prayer and worship.
9.   Be an example of hospitality.
10.   Be a person of faith with a positive attitude.
11.   Be a support to those preaching by taking notes and saying amen.
12.   Be approachable and available after all church services.

The Set Man must recognize and overcome these common leadership problems. To protect the vision of the church, he should instruct the leadership team to guard against these pitfalls.

CHAPTER FIVE

MOSES: THE SET MAN MODEL

Highlights

- Solitary leadership causes undue strain.

- A refusal to delegate stifles would-be leaders.

- The pastor of a growing church must move from hands-on to managerial shepherding.

- Divide big jobs into smaller tasks, then delegate the tasks and more can be done.

Like most who are called to the pastorate, Moses had a heart for his people. Like most congregations, the people had many needs--or should I say problems!? Finding the balance between these two factors always requires wisdom, foresight, and the ability to delegate authority.

A senior pastor must first understand the ministry gift God has given him before he can release the gift to others. Moses' dilemma and his method of solving it provides valuable insight for us.

. . . .

Good men should not kill themselves from excess work, even in God's service.

. . . .

How valuable is a little common sense! Here is Moses, trained and educated in Egypt, a man with all the credentials. Yet to overcome his pastoral problems, he must take self-evident advice from a mere man of the desert, his own father-in-law.

In Exodus 18:13-18 and Numbers 11:10-17 we have the dilemma and the answers for that dilemma. Moses, the Set Man over Israel, the senior pastor of the Israelite congregation, had too many problems for one man to handle. In Moses' problem we see the folly of solitary leadership.

Solitary leadership causes undue strain upon the solitary man. Wicked men sometimes kill themselves from excess pleasure. Good men should not kill themselves from excess work, even in the service of God. Many great lives are lost in the church through excessive toil.

It is a principle sufficiently evident in the infirmity of man, that he can not give himself incessantly to labor. Overwork can become a form of suicide. It is as much our duty to relax when we have overtaxed our strength, as it is to persevere when that strength is sufficient.

The experience of Moses teaches us that a man who will not delegate authority stifles would-be leaders, people who could help the leader and the rest of the congregation as well. It leaves unused a vast number of able men and women quite equal to the task, quite able to do the work at hand. The common congregation has many unsuspected abilities.

The words spoken to Moses by his father-in-law were words of wisdom that God Himself had put into the mouth of Jethro. Jethro said to Moses, "You will surely wear yourself out. This thing is too much for you. You are not able to perform it by yourself...The thing that you do is not good. The task is too heavy."

· ·

Moses had to move from being a shepherd to a rancher.

· ·

These are words which all of us need to hear as the Set Man or senior pastor of a church. Those who function over departments in a church or ministry also need to listen.

As his responsibilities grew, Moses had to move from being a shepherd to a rancher. I don't mean he lost his shepherd's heart or touch, but he had to change his philosophy of leadership. A shepherd pastor cares for people with a personal hands-on relationship. He counsels the people, leads the people, preaches to the people, prays for people, visits people, etc. He is basically an on-the-job shepherd.

As the church grows, a senior pastor must move from hands-on shepherding to more managerial shepherding. This is what I call the rancher model. He assumes the role of leadership and management with administration of the vision by delegation and wise leadership.

The job can be divided into many smaller tasks, with someone responsible for each task. That way we can do more, and we can do it better.

Moses' responsibility as the Set Man fell into five areas: (1) Intercessory Prayer, (2) Biblical Instruction, (3) Providing Qualified Leaders, (4) Handling Conflicts, and (5) Bringing Spiritual Breakthrough.

Intercession

> Listen now to my voice; I will give you counsel, and God will be with you: Stand before God for the people, so that you may bring the difficulties to God (Exodus 18:19).

Moses prayed for Israel, interceding between the people and God. In Exodus 17:9-16 he intercedes for Israel as they battle against Amalek. It was through Moses' intercession that the Amalekites were defeated.

Here is one of the great lessons of leadership. Most of our victories will come upon our knees, not on our office chairs. We must first learn to storm the throne of God before we can storm the gates of the enemy.

Wesley said, "Bear up the hands that hang down, by faith and prayer support the tottering knees. Have you any days of fasting and prayer? Storm the throne of grace and persevere therein, and mercy will come down."

· ·

There are no shortcuts. We must wait on God.

· ·

Oh that we might catch a vision today of the power of an intercessory leader! There is no man on earth more mighty than one who knows how to prevail with God and how to free those treasures in His hand that they might be bestowed in blessing, who knows how to rock the very fortresses of hell and the strongholds of Satan, loosing the captives and bringing them out.

Isaiah 59:16 says, "the Lord wondered that there was no intercessor," no one to intervene. An intercessor is one who intervenes between God and others, whether individual, church, community or nation.

A leader will never learn how to become an intercessor simply by reading books about prayer and intercession. He will never learn to intercede until he begins to pray and intercede. He must have a daily, diligent discipline in the fear of God, spending time in unhurried waiting on God in the sanctuary, learning in the secret place the wonderful ways of God. There are no shortcuts. He must wait on God, then God can begin to deal with those deep things within us which hinder the movement of God's Spirit.

E.M. Bounds states, "Prayer ascends by fire. Flame gives prayer access as well as wings, acceptance as well as energy. There is no incense without fire, no prayer without flame."

Through intercession the Set Man begins to see clearly the vision for the congregation. It is through intercession that the Set Man begins to discern those upon whom God has put a leadership call, which needs to be developed.

This is a day when God is giving vision, but only as we spend time in the prayer room waiting on God. Intercession is not rushing into God's presence with a long list of things we want God to do for us. Intercession is not bringing our pastoral programs before God, getting through with the business and on with something else. Intercession is the slow, painful process of waiting on God and hearing from God, spending time in His presence and being still before Him.

· ·

The pathway of the intercessor is a pathway of pain.

· ·

Intercession is not only spending time with God and understanding God, but it is allowing God to put within the Set Man a spiritual burden for the congregation and for the vision. The pathway of the intercessor is a pathway of pain—not physical pain but spiritual pain. The more you pastor the more pain you will feel, the pain of people's problems, the pain of poor decisions, the pain of relational hazards. There is much pain in the leadership role as the Set Man. It is only through intercession that pain can be turned to forgiveness and released to the congregation.

> I have set watchmen upon thy walls, O Jerusalem, who shall never hold their peace day nor night. Ye that make mention of the Lord, keep not silence and give Him no rest until He establish and until He make Jerusalem a praise in the earth (Isaiah 62:6-7).

It is through this kind of intercession that the church is established and becomes a praise in the earth. It is through intercession that the anointing of God is released; and it is the anointing that breaks the yoke (See Isaiah 10:27).

Through intercession we receive a realization that discernment is the mark of the mature church, that we might see into the spiritual realm as God sees. As Elijah says in II Kings 6:17, "Lord I pray, open his eyes that he may see." Intercession is the force that touches the heart, that moves the hand, that changes the world.

It is the first job of the Set Man to pray and intercede. "Ye shall be for the people a representative before God." Bringing the people before God is the job of the Set Man.

CHAPTER SIX

MOSES:
TEACHING THE WORD
OF GOD

Highlights

- We need men able to instruct, inspire, and stimulate the people with the pure Word of God.

- Do away with superficial preaching that lacks depth of feeling.

- Feeding the Word of God to the church is the central task and responsibility of all shepherds.

- The authority to lead is found in the authority to feed.

Moses instructed Israel. He inspired and stimulated the people through teaching of the Word of God, laying out the statutes and ordinances.

And you will teach them the statutes and the laws, and show them the way in which they must walk and the work they must do (Exodus 18:20).

A church can walk in the paths of the Lord only if it is taught properly.

Now it shall come to pass in the latter days that the mountain of the Lord's house shall be established on the top of the mountains, and shall be exalted above the hills; and all nations shall flow to it (Isaiah 2:2,3).

Before moving the people forward, a Set Man learns to first lay down the track, to chart the course. Following the Word of God, the church finds rest in growth.

. . . .

When sheep are hungry every bitter thing tastes sweet.

. . . .

A Set Man must become a Word man, totally baptized in the living Word of God and able to communicate it. In I Corinthians 11:23 Paul says, "For

I have received of the Lord that which also I delivered unto you." First he received. Then he delivered. To be a productive Set Man you must have the ability to receive a Word from the Lord and to deliver that Word to the congregation.

Isaiah 33:18 asks the question, "Where is the receiver?" The question is relevant today. Look at the different styles of preaching and what is being preached in the pulpits of many. Where are the receivers? Where are those who receive a fresh Word, fresh revelation by the Spirit of God?

II Timothy 2:15 says to "be diligent to present yourself approved to God, a worker who does not need to be ashamed, rightly dividing the Word of Truth." Study is work. It is labor. Like craftsmen making something worthy of praise, we are to be men who rightly divide the Word of Truth.

Some err on the side of depending too much on spiritual revelation without hard work and proper exegesis, using proper hermeneutics. Others err on the side of study and research, using proper hermeneutics and exegesis without the Spirit of the Lord.

Proverbs 25:2 says, "It is the glory of God to conceal a matter, but the glory of kings is to search out a matter." Our responsibility is to do the searching and the Holy Spirit will do the revealing.

Proverbs 27:7-8 says, "to a hungry soul every bitter thing is sweet." Around the world today, any erroneous cultic doctrine tastes sweet to spiritually hungry people. We need men like Moses who have the ability to instruct, inspire, and stimulate the people with the pure Word of God.

. . . .

We need to do away with routine professionalism.

. . . .

Psalm 30:1 says, "Out of the depths have I cried unto Thee." Break open the depth of your spirit and bring out the treasure both old and new to feed the people of God.

Do away with preaching that is superficial without depth of feeling, thought or judgment. Do away with routine professionalism and preaching that puts too much emphasis on experience, stories, and illustrations, shunning the true Word of God. Hear the fresh call of the Holy Spirit to return to proper exegesis of Scripture so we can proclaim the true, living Word of God, line upon line, here a little there a little.

In Acts 6:2 the apostles point out the problem all of us face today, serving too many tables instead of serving the Word of God. It is not seemly, desirable, or right that we should have to give up or neglect the Word of God in order to attend tables. What tables are you serving right now at the expense of the Word of God? The table of administration? The table of counseling? The table of recreation? The table of relationships? All of these are good, but at the expense of leaving the Word of God they will in due season harm the body of Christ.

Feeding the Word of God to the congregation is the central task and responsibility of all shepherds. Every Set Man should be a Word man. Acts 6:4 says, "We will give ourselves continually to prayer and to the ministry of the Word."

We are called to feed the flock of God with the Word of God.

So when they had eaten breakfast, Jesus said to Simon Peter, "Simon, son of Jonah, do you love Me more than these?" He said to Him, "Yes, Lord; You know that I love You." He said to him,

"Feed My lambs." He said to him again a second time, "Simon, son of Jonah, do you love Me?" He said to Him, "Yes, Lord; You know that I love You." He said to him, "Tend My sheep." He said to him the third time, "Simon, son of Jonah, do you love Me?" Peter was grieved because He said to him the third time, 'Do you love Me?' And he said to Him, "Lord, You know all things; You know that I love You." Jesus said to him, "Feed My sheep" (John 21:15-17).

The word *feed* used in these verses is translated from two different Greek words. *Bosko* means to feed, nourish, or provide food for the sheep. This speaks of the ministry of preaching, teaching, training, and even the prophetic.

. . . .

What tables are you serving at the expense of the Word of God?

. . . .

Poimaino means to act as a shepherd, to tend the sheep to watch over and care for the sheep. This speaks of the caring ministry of counseling, relating, visiting, loving, and caring.

The balanced ministry of the Set Man includes both *bosko* and *poimaino*. We cannot become only a *poimaino* man and neglect the *bosko*. Nor can we become a *bosko* man and neglect the *poimaino*. We must combine the two.

Therefore take heed to yourselves and to all the flock, among which the Holy Spirit has made you overseers, to shepherd the church of God which He purchased with His own blood (Acts 20:28).

Shepherd the flock of God which is among you, serving as overseers, not by constraint but willingly, not for dishonest gain but eagerly (I Peter 5:2).

And I will give you shepherds according to My heart, who will feed you with knowledge and understanding (Jeremiah 3:15).

"I will set up shepherds over them who will feed them; and they shall fear no more, nor be dismayed, nor shall they be lacking", says the Lord (Jeremiah 23:4).

Here are practical helpful hints for your Word ministry.

• Do not throw out classical systems of theology just because they are old.

• Follow logical order in establishing your theology, constructing your view with biblical theology which will have a great deal of influence upon your preaching ministry.

• Establish a proper skill of biblical exegesis. Be aware that your primary assumption of the Word of God will dramatically affect your results. The method of determining the biblical definition of a word in the Bible is the Bible usage of that word, not the linguistic meaning or cultural background only.

- Guard against developing an atomistic theology and atomistic approach to the Bible, addressing only certain parts of the Word of God rather than the whole Word of God. Don't stay in a rut by trying to make a whole theology out of one atom.

- Find the necessary key principles of biblical interpretation for the Scriptures you are studying. Take time to use hermeneutics.

- Develop a thorough understanding of what happened on the cross, viewing the atonement, the suffering of Christ, the vicarious aspects of it, the surrendering aspects, the theological aspects. What really happened on the cross?

- Develop a greater awareness of biblical metaphors and images. Learn how to develop an occasional use of gospel handles. That is, a given text that might not contain the Gospel, but where you can see the Gospel. This is called a gospel handle.

The main business of preaching is to lift up Christ and to proclaim the Gospel. The Gospel can clearly be explained and illustrated in Scriptures where the gospel principle is evident even though the word gospel is not mentioned.

. . . .

The authority to lead is found in
the authority to feed.

. . . .

Learn how to use a single word from a text, such
as the word mountain, grace, law, man, lift. Use a
phrase such as cut it off, lift it up, pull forward. Or use
an entire sentence and just preach from one sentence.
"And He stayed where He was two more days." Why
does God delay? Is God late?

Use metaphors from a text such as Isaiah 22:23-
25–the peg or the nail. Here we see the redemption of
Jesus fixed as a nail in the wall, the picture of Christ
fixed as a peg, so is the redemptive work of God fixed,
immovable.

A Set Man must develop a superior feeding
ministry more than any other gift he has. The authority
to lead is found in the authority to feed.

CHAPTER SEVEN

MOSES:
PROVIDING
QUALIFIED LEADERS

Highlights

- The Set Man gathers and develops potential leaders.

- You risk gathering untested, unstable, unfaithful, and disloyal leaders; exploiting the church for their own purposes.

- Watch for those who are willing to serve in menial areas.

- Beware of those who are unable to keep confidences.

Moses was instructed to select a particular kind of person to stand with him and help bear the load. These were to be able men. The original Hebrew text alludes to the idea of having strength, power, or might; to be warlike and to display courage, valor; to be firm (See II Samuel 17:10).

> Moreover you shall select from all the people able men, such as fear God, men of truth, hating covetousness; and place such over them to be rulers of thousands, rulers of hundreds, rulers of fifties, and rulers of tens (Exodus 18:21).

> Then I will come down and talk with you there. I will take of the Spirit that is upon you and will put the same upon them; and they shall bear the burden of the people with you, that you may not bear it yourself alone (Numbers 11:17).

> Then the Lord came down in the cloud, and spoke to him, and took of the Spirit that was upon him, and placed the same upon the seventy elders; and it happened, when the Spirit rested upon them, that they prophesied, although they never did so again (Numbers 11:25).

Moses picked men who feared God--men who revered God. Fearing and proper living are closely related, almost synonymous. These men were to have a healthy respect for God and a holy life.

. . . .

Moses was to provide leaders the congregation could respect, trust and follow without fear.

. . . .

Moses was to choose men of truth who consistently kept their promises, men of their word, men of integrity. He chose men who hated covetousness and who were not moved by financial gain. He looked for men who had the spirit of wisdom, for wisdom is needed in every area of leadership, every area of life. They were to be men who were mature, respected, and proven in their ministry. They were to have a reputation that was established and accepted by the people.

Moses' responsibility was to provide leaders the congregation could respect, trust, and follow without fear. The church today needs qualified leadership to lead her to the victories of tomorrow.

Where does the Set Man find qualified leadership? Should the Set Man raise up his own or import them from a college or another like-natured church? If the pastor chooses to train his own, what methods should he use? What qualifications should the leader possess?

The Bible is the source book for all who train leaders and who endeavor to build healthy local churches. Concepts and principles of raising up local leaders should be established upon biblical premises.

. . . .

The Set Man has the responsibility
of gathering and developing good
leaders.

. . . .

In Philippians 2:20 Paul refers to the leader he
had raised up for the Ephesian church. "For I have no
man like-minded as Timothy." Other translations say,
"Of equal soul" or "as interested as I am in the people of
God." "For I have no one else as near to my own
attitude as my son, Timothy." "For I have no one else
of kindred spirit, no one like-disposed."

Paul was in prison. His ministry was limited, so
he had to trust someone. He put his trust in his son-in-
the-faith, Timothy. No one except Timothy would
handle problems, people, and pressure the way Paul,
himself, would handle them. Timothy was a man of
proven character and ministry, a true son in the gospel.
Timothy had what Paul called a "kindred spirit." He
was like-minded, equal in soul.

A Set Man has the responsibility to gather
potential leaders and to develop them to be good
leaders for the congregation. I Chronicles 12:22 says,
"Day by day men came to David until there was a great
army, an army of God." When you gather great leaders,
you have the beginning of a great church. Your leaders
will have the ability to carry on the work of God in
every department of the church just as you would as
the Holy Spirit would anoint you--and even better.

Jesus prayed all night before choosing the twelve
(Luke 6:12-13). When you gather leaders you take a
risk. This is one of the necessary risks of being a Set
Man. Fervent prayer is the only wise approach!

• **You risk gathering imposter leaders.**

Acts 28:3 says, "But when Paul had gathered a bundle of sticks and laid them on the fire, a viper came out because of the heat, and fastened on his hand."

Paul gathered sticks to build a fire to warm himself. But in the sticks there was a snake. As soon as the fire heated the snake, it struck out and attached itself to Paul's hand.

When we gather leaders we take a chance that in a pile of sticks there may be one snake. That snake may have enough will power to attach itself to your hand and poison you in the ministry.

Paul shook off the snake, and you can too. Isaiah 11:1-3 says we should learn to judge not by the natural eye or the natural ear. We must pray all night, like Jesus, who prayed for discernment in choosing the right leaders. It is possible to have more sticks than snakes, although at times it seems we have chosen more snakes than sticks.

• **You risk gathering untested leaders.**

Paul chose John Mark who failed him in a time of pressure.

Now when Paul and his party set sail from Paphos, they came to Perga in Pamphylia; and John, departing from them, returned to Jerusalem (Acts 13:13).

But Paul insisted that they should not take with them the one who had departed from them in Pamphylia, and had not gone with them to the work (Acts 15:38) .

Mark failed the team in a time of crisis. He vacillated and turned back. He let Paul dow... He revealed a character flaw. He was later restored to the leadership team after his character was developed.

Leaders take this kind of risk in choosing leaders who are untested and unproven. We might be surprised. We might be disappointed. Never be so disappointed that you refuse to restore a leader who had disappointed you. Keep developing them even when you do see their glaring weaknesses.

Get Mark and bring him with you, for he is useful to me for ministry (II Timothy 4:11).

• **You risk gathering unstable and unfaithful leaders.**

David had Ahithophel (II Samuel 15:12; 16:21; 17:23), Paul chose Demas.

Luke the beloved physician and Demas greet you (Colossians 4;14).

Demas was for a short time changed by Paul's presence. He was magnetized by Paul's magnetic ministry, but as soon as he was away from that magnet he went back to his own character and denied the way of Christ (See II Timothy 4:10). Demas is the mark of a disciple whose wavering impulse caused him to surrender the passion of sacrifice and sink in the swirling waters of the world.

- **You risk gathering disloyal leaders.**

Absalom was gifted with remarkable beauty, commanding presence, natural dignity, extraordinary graces, charm, and eloquence (II Samuel 14:25). Yet a treacherous nature was within him. Absalom had unresolved offenses which lead him to hate and betray David. His ego, pride, and selfishness led him to believe he could have anything he wanted and that he was a better leader than the great David, his own father. His disloyalty led him to a murderous plot toward his own family (II Samuel 15). He was willing to attack David so that his own egotistical spirit could be satisfied.

- **You risk gathering leaders who will exploit the local church for their own purposes, and will not care for the flock as a true shepherd would.**

The leader we all want has an unoffended heart, an uncomplaining heart that trusts God's ways, His unexplained dealings with the soul and his ordering of life. This kind of leader is rare.

We need leaders who are birthed into the main elements of the local church vision, principles, and philosophies. They need to be birthed into the vision of the house (Proverbs 29:18), the principles of the house (II Chronicles 4:20; I Chronicles 15:13), the philosophy of the house, the standards of the house, the doctrines of the house, the procedures of the house and the spirit of the house. As the Bible says in Genesis 14:14, "Abraham's servants, who became warriors, were trained in his own house."

The birthing process for team members requires a spiritual identification with the local church. As the vision and principles of the local church are set forth, they must be assimilated into the team member's spirit, not just his mind. A spiritual illumination must take place resulting in a teachable spirit and a changed leader.

. . . .

Watch for those who are willing to serve in menial areas.

. . . .

The Holy Spirit will illuminate the mind of the Set Man as the team is being formed. The Lord will lay on the heart of the senior pastor those to train and raise up in the local church. Look for stability of character, someone with a settled, untroubled, and unoffended heart. A positive identification mark would be faithfulness in all areas of living--faithfulness in small things, in natural things, and in things belonging to another man (Luke 16:10-12).

A humble leader will respond properly when corrected. If pride is involved there will be reaction and irritation continually as you try to raise up a leader who will not take correction.

Watch for those who are willing to serve in menial areas, not just in the areas they choose. They should show a willingness to serve in any area of the church that has need. A man who manipulates himself into a place of leadership without serving is a leader who will mutilate the body of Christ.

A high level of personal integrity is of utmost importance. A leader must take his own words seriously. He is a man to whom a promise creates an obligation which must be met, a person who will fulfill his vow and his commitments.

Leaders who have identified with the spirit of the Set Man and the spirit of the house also respond to the preaching and teaching from the pulpit. If a leader does not take notes, say amen, smile, or show a response, surely there should be some discussion about the person's love for the preaching.

As a leader is birthed in the local church, he will have a genuine love for people. He will stay after services and mingle with the people. People will want to be with him and gather around him at all public gatherings, potlucks, home fellowship meetings and leadership meetings. His sensitivity to the needs of others births in others a love for that leader.

. . . .

Beware of those who are unable to keep confidences.

. . . .

Choose people who have successful family and occupational relationships. Watch out for those who have an inability to keep confidences and who are hasty in their decision making. If a person continues to make poor judgment calls and poor decisions even after they have been warned and taught concerning those areas, that person will ultimately hurt the church.

One who is emotionally unstable in situations that cause pressure, will also cause emotional problems in the church. Not only should you look at the leader himself, but also consider the wife. Emotional instability will cause pressure in both the home and their leadership area.

If a person is pushing for promotion and recognition it will come out in little ways before it is clearly manifested. Notice if he is always siding with people who make wrong decisions, or who promote wrong concepts. If he regularly justifies himself and shifts blame away from himself, this should warn you not to raise him up as a leader.

All potential ministry team members must encounter the revealing fire of God. Fire reveals the true nature of the potential leader. Until a leader goes through the fire he is an unknown factor in the leadership team (See Leviticus 1:7-17; Matthew 3:11-12; I Corinthians 3:13; I Peter 1:7; Hebrews 12:24).

CHAPTER EIGHT

MOSES HANDLING CONFLICTS IN THE CHURCH

Highlights

- A Set Man who does not know how to handle conflicts will continually have them in his church.

- Not all conflict is negative.

- All leadership should be underneath pushing up.

- Maturity is evidenced when a problem is encountered without overreaction, retaliation or criticism.

Moses handled the hard cases. In the local church, conflicts are the hard cases.

> And let them judge the people at all times. Then it will be that every great matter they shall bring to you, but every small matter they themselves shall judge. So it will be easier for you, for they will bear the burden with you (Exodus 18:22).

All churches in every part of the world experience the devastating effects of disagreement, discord, and conflict. The early church in the New Testament encountered several such problems and survived. The main problem in most churches usually relates back to an unresolved leadership conflict or an unresolved congregational conflict.

God gave Moses the ability to handle the conflicts that arose in the nation of Israel. The Set Man today has the anointing of the Holy Spirit and the wisdom of God to handle the various conflicts which surface in the church. A Set Man who does not know how to handle various conflicts will continually have little fires burning in his church.

· ·

Not all conflict is negative.

· ·

Conflict can make us hard or soft, bitter or better. It can make us lose confidence and fearful to take initiative when we see trouble because we are afraid of what might happen. Conflict strengthens our character. The more conflict we have the more we will pray, learn the Word of God, and keep humility as the canopy over our lives.

Conflict makes us examine and purify our motives. Conflict reveals faults and flaws in ourselves and in the church which otherwise would not have been revealed. Conflict teaches us spiritual endurance and spiritual carefulness. Sometimes it even jolts us into the will of God when we weren't intending it to jolt us anywhere. Not all conflict is negative. There are times when the Lord shakes the church and allows conflict to come so He can make needed changes.

Webster's dictionary defines conflict as "a striking together, a contest; to fight, contest, to clash, incompatibility; to be in opposition, sharp disagreement; emotional disturbance resulting from a clash."

The Greek word *agon* was used to identify the place where the Greeks assembled for the Olympic Games and watched the contest by the athletes. This word came to mean "struggle" or "combat." *Agon* is translated five different ways in the New Testament. It is translated in the New Testament "conflict" in Philippians 1:30, "contention" in I Thessalonians 2:2; "fight" in I Timothy 6:12; "race" in Hebrews 12:1; and "agony" in Luke 22:44.

Conflict is a sister to contention. These two dwell together and grow together whenever they are not handled properly. In Acts 15:39 the early church saw sharp contention between its leadership (See also Proverbs 18:18; I Corinthians 1:11; Proverbs 23:30).

The word *contention* has the idea of quarreling, especially rivalry or wrangling as in the church at Corinth, or to have sharp feeling or emotion towards someone that affects our irritation level. Contention carries with it the idea of strife, or to be a lover of strife. It signifies the eagerness to contend. Where there is contention and conflict there is also strife and discord (Proverbs 6:16-19).

Here are some of the leadership sources of conflict:

- When there is an inconsistency in the practicing of biblical principles which are clearly established in the local church.

- When the leadership violates standards and attitudes taught to the people.

- When leadership presumptuously declares a vision or direction from the Lord and then aborts the direction to move in another direction without explanation.

- When leadership avoids, procrastinates, or ignores the need to confront those who are sowing seeds of contention and then does not properly handle the problem.

- When a senior pastor violates his own standards and wisdom in choosing unqualified leadership to serve the people, thus causing great confusion.

- When the pastor or a staff leader handles an explosive situation in haste, without prayer and without considering the ramifications of his actions or decisions.

- When leadership will not consistently practice the principle of forgiveness as taught in Matthew 18, allowing offenses to grow in the church and in the leaders.

- When the senior pastor violates the spirit of team ministry by acting independently of the elders or staff leadership in making major decisions which will affect the whole body.

In Acts 15 we see three basic principles which were used by the leadership in handling conflicts. First, we see the principle of effective communication with an honest heart and a teachable spirit (Acts 15:1-4,6). Second, we see the principle of the leadership coming together to consider the matter before they spoke to the congregation (Acts 15:6). Third, we see the principle of gathering all the facts from the parties involved.

These three principles will work in any conflict in the local church. Effective communication takes a lot of time and a lot of work. Gathering facts can be tedious and painful, yet without all the facts, you risk multiplying the conflict rather than solving it.

Here are some practical tips in handling conflicts in the leadership team or in the local church.

- The principle of refraining from hasty decisions.

- The principle of immediate action with grace.

- The principle of allowing for human failure.

- The principle of not repeating half-truths.

- The principle of love looking for the best in people.

- The principle of disciplining carnal impulses and negative reactions.

- The principle of handling vain imaginations.

- The principle of realizing that we are at war with a spiritual adversary, the devil.

- The principle of allowing some differences in methodology.

- The principle of dealing with root problems, not just manifestations.

The foot-washing service in John 13 provides insight into handling conflicts. Three things happened in this chapter.

First, Jesus laid aside his garments. The mature servant is willing to lay aside his reputation or his position status to deal with a problem.

. . . .

All leadership should be underneath pushing up.

. . . .

Many times we have to lay aside our titles and our positions to speak lovingly to one another and not allow any of these things to intimidate people we deal with. A mature leader knows that in dealing with conflict he must expose himself and be deeply sincere and honest with people.

Second, Jesus girded himself with a towel. This is servant dress. A true leader will gird himself with a servant's attitude. All leadership should be underneath pushing up. All leadership should take the servant's mentality, the servant's attitude continually, in every situation.

Even when you are right and you have been accused of wrong, take the servant's attitude. When you are in a place where you can retaliate, take the servant's attitude. When you are in a place where you can bring vengeance on someone, remember the servant's towel. The robe of the servant is not the white collar or the title. It is the attitude of the servant.

Third, Jesus washed their feet. This was the function of a servant. This shows Christ's humility and how unselfish He was concerning His own reputation. True humility expresses itself not in unfavorable comparisons of ourselves with others, but in wholehearted devotion to the interests of others.

I Peter 5:5 in the Concordant Literal translation says, "Tie on humility like a dress fastened with strings." Jesus showed the disciples how to minister one to another, and how to prepare themselves for conflicts which would arise within the team and within the church. We can do this only when we wear the servant's towel.

Washing one another with a humble spirit and the power of the Holy Spirit becomes a key to relationships within the leadership team. Washing by the Holy Spirit is the evidence of maturity and the key to team success.

We are responsible to lay aside our garments while washing. We are responsible to clothe ourselves with a servant's towel. We are responsible to wash our brother even when he initially rejects us and does not want us to wash him (like Peter who did not want Christ to wash his feet). We are responsible to wash ourselves first to make sure we speak from a clean heart and spirit (Psalm 51:2,7; John 9:7; Acts 16:33).

Many conflicts must be washed from our hearts and from the leadership team. The Set Man must set the example of being a servant with a humble spirit, washing others and responding to those who come to wash him.

We sometimes bruise one another with our tongues, passing on half-truths or saying things that harm one another. These things need to be washed out of our spirit, and washed from the leadership and from the church. At times we hold and hide resentments which come from offenses or disappointments. We must release these in the power of the Holy Spirit and ask the Lord Jesus to heal us.

Blind spots cause us to stumble and make wrong decisions. As we form a leadership team, it is with the help of others that these blind spots can be washed out of our lives to save us from destruction.

· ·

Maturity is evidenced when a problem is encountered without overreaction, retaliation or criticism.

· ·

We might have past failures in relationships with other team members. Not all relationships go smoothly. Sometimes we remember people the wrong way. We think of the last conflict we had with them or the last thing they said to us that was not as wholesome as it should have been. We may judge people on past failures in relationships. Sometimes we make hasty judgments against other leaders' decisions or procedures.

Maturity is evidenced when a problem is encountered without overreaction, retaliation, criticism, taking it personally, or allowing a fixation on that issue. May the Holy Spirit give every leader the kind of spirit that allows us to wash one another and build a strong team in spite of the conflicts we endure.

CHAPTER NINE

MOSES: SPIRITUAL ADVANCEMENT OF THE CONGREGATION

Highlights

- The spiritual advancement of the church depends upon leaders capable of lifting up the rod and breaking through the obstacles at hand.

- The Set Man is the key to moving the people of God forward.

- Don't hold too tightly to your ministry. It belongs to God.

The spiritual advancement of the church depends upon spiritual leaders who are capable of breaking through the obstacles at hand. Moses carried a rod, which God turned into an instrument that helped to free and to lead the nation of Israel.

> And the Lord said to Moses, "Why do you cry to Me? Tell the children of Israel to go forward" (Exodus 14:15).

> Then Moses answered and said, "But suppose they will not believe me or listen to my voice; suppose they say, 'The Lord has not appeared to you.' " So the Lord said to him, "What is that in your hand?" And he said, "A rod." And He said, "Cast it on the ground." So he cast it on the ground, and it became a serpent; and Moses fled from it (Exodus 4:1-3).

The rod speaks of the Set Man's confirmation by God of his spiritual gifting to lead the church forward at all times. The Set Man then places his confidence in the fact that he has been equipped and called to lead.

The person with the rod is the key to moving the people of God forward. Israel was baptized or immersed during the leadership of Moses (I Corinthians 10:2). No Moses--no advancement!

. . . .

The Set Man is the key to moving
the people of God forward.

. . . .

The following Scriptures show the rod ministry
at work:

●   To do signs and wonders.

    And you shall take this rod in your hand, with
    which you shall do the signs (Exodus 4:17).

●   To open a way where there is no way.

    But lift up your rod, and stretch out your hand
    over the sea and divide it. And the children of
    Israel shall go on dry ground through the midst
    of the sea (Exodus 14:16).

●   To release water in the wilderness, refreshing the
    people of God.

    And the Lord said to Moses, "Go on before the
    people, and take with you some of the elders of
    Israel. Also take in your hand your rod with
    which you struck the river, and go" (Exodus
    17:5).

●   To secure victories in the heat of warfare.

    And Moses said to Joshua, "Choose us some men
    and go out, fight with Amalek. Tomorrow I will

stand on the top of the hill with the rod of God in my hand" (Exodus 17:9).

- To provide food for the flock of God.

  Shepherd Your people with Your staff, the flock of Your heritage, who dwell solitarily in a woodland, in the midst of Carmel; let them feed in Bashan and Gilead, as in days of old (Micah 7:14).

- To rule with balanced power and authority.

  He who has an ear, let him hear what the Spirit says to the churches. To him who overcomes I will give to eat from the tree of life, which is in the midst of the Paradise of God (Revelation 2:7).

  And she bore a male Child who was to rule all nations with a rod of iron. And her Child was caught up to God and to His throne (Revelation 12:5).

  Now out of His mouth goes a sharp sword, that with it He should strike the nations. And He Himself will rule them with a rod of iron. He Himself treads the winepress of the fierceness and wrath of Almighty God (Revelation 19:15).

- To measure the house of God, to build according to divine pattern.

  Then I was given a reed like a measuring rod. And the angel stood, saying, "Rise and measure the temple of God, the altar, and those who worship there. But leave out the court which is outside the temple, and do not measure it, for it has been given to the Gentiles. And they will tread the holy city underfoot for forty-two months" (Revelation 11:1-2).

• To correct and set the house of God in order.

What do you want? Shall I come to you with a rod, or in love and a spirit of gentleness? (I Corinthians 4:21).

The Set Man is to lift up his rod. Do not let your own defeats and questions cause you to reject the divine provision in the rod God has given you. God anoints the office, not just the man. Some people will rise against the methods or personality of the Set Man, not understanding that God honors the office and the man. With the calling to be a Set Man over a congregation comes the authority and honor of God to lead that congregation.

Lift up your rod! Take confidence in your calling, in your office! God will make a way where there is no way. God will provide refreshing water for the flock in the midst of desert storms. Used properly with faith and humility the rod results in great benefits for the people of God.

Moses was told to "cast it down" (Exodus 4:3). This may speak of our need to learn how to relinquish our ministry back to God. All that we have belongs to the Lord. Don't hold too tightly to your "rod." It belongs to God. Cast it down before His feet in an attitude of gratefulness, knowing He has given the rod and He can take it back.

We are told in Exodus 4:3 that the rod "became a serpent." This may speak to us of the evil potential of all our talents and ministries when not kept by God. Each Set Man has the potential to become a serpent. Serpentology can replace our theology and our integrity.

. . . .

Don't hold too tightly to your ministry. It belongs to God.

. . . .

If God would give every Set Man a glimpse of how wicked he could be without the mercy and grace of God abiding in him and on him, it would change his whole ministry forever.

Moses is told to "pick it up by the tail". The serpent then turns into a rod again. Picking a snake up by the tail is opposite to the natural wisdom of man. You cannot control or protect yourself if you pick up the serpent by the tail. God help us to understand we must handle the rod God has placed in our hands with great carefulness and wisdom. The rod is used to break through any seemingly impossible obstacles that stand in the way of spiritual advancement.

> But lift up your rod, and stretch out your hand over the sea and divide it. And the children of Israel shall go on dry ground through the midst of the sea (Exodus 14:16).

Israel needed a breakthrough. A breakthrough may be defined as a spiritual victory that removes longstanding obstacles and releases the people of God into a new realm of spiritual blessing and freedom. Moses lifted his rod and divided the obstacle.

The word *divide* in Exodus 14:16 means a cleaving that results in a bursting forth, a striking with great force so as to break through, opening what was shut, the forcefulness of splitting a tree, or of troops breaking into a walled city, thus removing all obstacles.

We must not become weary of using the rod of authority against stubborn obstacles. A stone cutter hammers a rock a hundred times without a crack showing in it. Yet, at the one hundred and first blow it splits in two. It was not the one blow that split it, but all that had gone before! With God's anointing on our rod, we will break through every Red Sea, every obstacle before us!

> So David went to Baal Perazim, and there he defeated them. He said, "As waters break out, the Lord has broken out against my enemies before me." So that place was called Baal Perazim (II Samuel 5:20).

> So the three mighty men broke through the Philistine lines, drew water from the well near the gate of Bethlehem and carried it back to David (II Samuel 23:16a).

An early church bishop wrote this prayer that may be applicable to every leader:

> "Since you O Lord have appointed this blind guide to lead them Your people, for their sakes, Lord, if not for mine, teach him whom You have made to be their teacher, lead him whom You have bidden to lead them, rule him who is their ruler."

CHAPTER TEN

THE SET MAN GIFT MIX

Highlights

- The senior pastor's ministry affects every aspect of church life.

- An apostle/pastor plants churches and fathers other pastors.

- A prophet/pastor inspires faith for signs and wonders.

- Missions and outreach surround an evangelist/pastor.

- A teacher/pastor can grow large, well-balanced churches.

The ministry expression of the senior pastor is of utmost importance for all decision making, vision setting, and feeding of the church.

The Set Man gift mix may be a combination of any of the five ascension gift ministries, graces, and other spiritual gifts.

> And He Himself gave some to be apostles, some prophets, some evangelists, and some pastors and teachers, for the equipping of the saints for the work of ministry, for the edifying of the body of Christ (Ephesians 4:11-12).

These are the post-ascension gift ministries. After Christ descended and ascended He gave the church these gifts.

The five-fold--apostle, prophet, evangelist, pastor and teacher--is for the perfecting, equipping and building up of the body of Christ. The end result of these ministries is to bring the church to the unity of faith and unto a perfect or mature man.

The apostle is sent forth with authority to faithfully represent the purposes and intentions of the Sender. The prophet is a mouthpiece for God. The evangelist announces the good news of the Gospel and equips other people to do the same. The pastor feeds and tends the sheep. The teacher instructs others, presenting truth in systematic sequences.

The gift mix of the Apostolic Set Man

The apostle/pastor gift mix produces a strong apostolic foundation, apostolic vision, and an apostolic leadership team. Church planting and the fathering of other pastors is evident in the church. A strong emphasis on doctrine and principles of biblical structure make for a very strong, healthy church.

. . . .

The apostle/pastor sees beyond needs to spiritual truths which are needed to establish a strong church.

. . . .

However, at times these churches may look rigid and seem to lack inspirational ministry. They usually focus on the basics and the foundation to build longevity into the church rather than on the inspirational ministries which are based on a felt-need mentality. Some people mistakenly think the apostle/pastor does not have the heart to meet the needs of the people. Usually he sees beyond the needs to the spiritual truths which need to be established to build a strong, long-lasting church.

The gift mix of the Prophetic Set Man

A church led by a prophet/pastor tends to be a more inspirational, signs and wonders, faith-type church with much expectation in the air. It usually is not strong in doctrine and principles and may be weak in administration. Discipleship often occurs by osmosis instead of by well-thought-out strategy. The prophetic

Set Man needs to raise up leaders around him with administrative and teaching gifts to add ministries which he himself is not adding to the church.

The prophetic Set Man is usually one who has a long-range vision and ministers the Word of God through types, shadows, symbols, parables and stories in setting forth the vision.

The gift mix of the Evangelistic Set Man

The evangelist/pastor usually produces a growing church because of the focus and strength of the gifted lead man. His charisma, and need-oriented teaching with great worship produces an electrified atmosphere of faith and spiritual expectation. Missions and outreach usually become the heartbeat of the church.

. . . .

An evangelist/pastor may gather great crowds, but may not nurture them into becoming strong Christians.

. . . .

Possible weaknesses would be shallow preaching and a lack of cohesiveness in the church life and membership. An evangelist/ pastor may gather great crowds, but may not nurture them into a strong foundational Christianity as an apostle/Set Man could. The evangelist/Set Man should raise up other leaders around him with apostolic and teaching gifts to nurture the church in the areas of need.

The gift mix of the Pastoral Set Man

The combination of a dominant pastoral and motivational ministry results in well-fed, well-cared-for sheep. The pastoral gift mix operating in the Set Man will be evidenced in his caring and maintaining of the flock more than the visionary-type leader. Administration, a safe budget, and a well-kept flock is his dream. The church may stay small, but usually it is safe and guaranteed to last. This kind of a ministry usually develops a great cell system in the church and a lot of training for those who do pastoral counseling. The church may be one that is more in-looking than out-looking.

The gift mix of the Teacher Set Man

The teacher/pastor mix has the capacity to grow large, well-balanced churches. His gifting sets in motion a powerful chemistry which results in depth of spiritual experience and breadth of spiritual security. This person usually is a good communicator, systematic, and a series preacher. This, combined with a love for people, warm personality, and the ability to structure for shepherding is a dynamic mix.

If anything, this church could possibly have too much material put forth on Sundays. He gives a lot of points, a lot of instruction with not enough evangelism and inspiration. To strengthen weak areas, the teaching Set Man can equip the church and raise up inspirational ministries to bring that church into health.

CHAPTER ELEVEN

THE SET MAN MINISTRY PROFILE

Highlights

- Staff your weaknesses.

- Spiritual health of the people is a long-term obligation.

- Motivate and equip church members.

- Generate and sustain a common purpose.

- Confronting, adjusting, and removing leaders.

- The Set Man must interpret culture.

- Leading by support--a servant style of leadership.

The leadership style of the Set Man is the manner he uses to express his values and execute his ministry. Leadership style refers to each person's distinctive approach.

The senior minister or Set Man may function in some or all of the ministry expressions. He may do some things better than others. Usually a balanced leadership team is built to strengthen the weaker side of the senior pastor. The rule of thumb is: Never staff your strengths; always staff your weaknesses.

The Set Man as preacher

The Set Man holds fast to the faithful Word, exhorts in sound doctrine and refutes those who contradict the truth.

The Word of God is the basis of his teaching. The preacher should do the exegesis of his text carefully, using proper hermeneutics. Preaching should feed the saints and equip them to compose a strong, healthy church.

The Set Man as prophetic

The prophetic Set Man exhorts, encourages, and urges people toward set goals.

He corrects reproves, rebukes, and exhorts people to get back on track to the God-given goal when they have gone astray. The prophetic man can see beyond the present into the future and equip the people to walk in faith.

The effective congregation holds a clear authentic purpose in common commitment among its members. It also pursues that purpose through a well-reasoned strategy. Its activities or programs are related to its purpose through a carefully worked out rationale. Purpose functions as the touchstone for every thought, decision, plan, or action, and it provides the overall perspective from which each of these can be viewed.

The Set Man as watchman

The watchman hears the sound of the trumpet and rightly discerns the message. He must respond to the warning of the trumpet if he is to deliver his own soul.

. . . .

The watchman must be on the alert for "little things" that destroy a local church.

. . . .

After the watchman hears the trumpet he sounds the alarm and alerts the people to coming danger (See Hebrews 13:17; Numbers 10:4; Ezekiel 3:17; 33:1-9; Acts 20:28-31; Jeremiah 31:6). The watchman must be on the alert for the "little" things that destroy a local church.

The Scriptures speak of "little foxes" in Song of Solomon 2:15; "little indifference" in Proverbs 6:10 and 24:30-33; "little folly" in Ecclesiastes 10:1,6; "little leaven" in Galatians 5:9 and I Corinthians 5:6; "little unfaithfulness" in Luke 16:10; and "little member" (the tongue) in James 3:1-5.

The Set Man as pastoral

The Set Man provides the congregation with qualified leaders who help the senior pastor care for the church.

Senior pastors should pastor the leadership using the Paretto principle (80/20) as the guideline for pastoring the entire congregation. Paretto was an eighteenth century French economist who taught that success was best attained by business owners spending 80 percent of their time with 20 percent of their most influential people. The pastor assumes long-term responsibility for the spiritual health of the flock.

The Set Man as manager

The Set Man finds and marshals resources to develop ways and means of organizing people and programs to achieve God-set goals and visions.

He establishes policies and goals keeping counter-productive processes from weakening the dynamics of the local church.

. . . .

The goal of the Set Man should be
to make every Christian a minister.

. . . .

The Set Man as equipper

The Set Man sets goals for a congregation in accordance with the will of God.

He works to instill those goals in the people and looks for the people to embrace the goals as their own.

He works to motivate and equip the people to do their respective parts in accomplishing the congregational goals.

The goal of the Set Man should be to make every Christian a minister. Elton Trueblood stated it powerfully: "If the average church should suddenly take seriously the notion that every lay member--man or woman--is really a minister of Christ, we could have something like a revolution in a very short time."

Thomas Gillespie says in His Book *The Laity in Biblical Perspective* "Mobilization takes place if the nonclergy are willing to move up, if the clergy are willing to move over, and if all God's people are willing to move out." [5]

The Set Man as visionary

The Set Man generates, communicates, and sustains commonality of purpose.

He can fire the imagination and create a sense of dedication for a vision which motivates followers into effective, meaningful service. He guards the identity and direction of the congregation, clarifying and emphasizing purpose. The visionary is a spiritual pacesetter. The visionary develops strategies for implementing the mission of the church and constantly generates momentum to achieve goals.

The Set Man as leader

The Set Man causes the church to progress by emphasizing, clarifying, and reminding people of their purpose.

He keeps an objective in the spotlight, showing people how to merge their efforts to accomplish their common goals. He is a catalyst who helps individuals to harmonize their abilities as the body of Christ, helping people to strengthen their purposefulness through a growing commitment to Christ and His kingdom.

The Set Man as team refiner.

The Set Man confronts, adjusts, or removes leaders who hold an official position of leadership but do not lead. A non-functioning leader transmits stagnation. This kind of "foot-dragging" may indicate that a leader secretly wants to hinder progress by quietly opposing ideas or decisions. Whether this error is accidental or intentional, the Set Man is right to oppose it. When taking decisive action like this, leadership should follow this maxim: "If you kick, be sure you kick toward the goal." Leadership must be careful to make a positive contribution to the right goal, and not to react in a counter-productive way.

The Set Man as a risk taker/innovator

The Set Man welcomes change and is excited about the opportunities it brings. Usually he is an optimist. He is optimistic about the future, a trailblazer, pioneer, paradigm shifter, risk taker, and of course a good problem solver. He is not content merely to imagine the future but wants to create and possess a future. An innovator seeks to translate vision into reality and has the drive and persistence to do it. He creates and implements ideas successfully. A breakthrough idea represents a stretching of a leader's abilities, skills, and energies to make the idea manifest in the church or in the kingdom of God.

. . . .

An innovator seeks to translate vision into reality.

. . . .

A businessman attended a seminar conducted by a self-made millionaire. The millionaire had made money by speculating in commodities. During the lecture a spectator stood and asked the millionaire, "Didn't you realize all this speculation was risky and that you could have lost every penny you had?" The millionaire said, "Why yes, I did." The man then asked, "Why did you continue to speculate?" The millionaire said, "I don't know exactly why. I just know I was willing to take the risk." The man, now a little irate snapped, "Well, I'm not!" The millionaire smiled and said, "That may be why I'm giving this lecture, and you're paying for it!"

The Set Man as team catalyst

The Set Man draws together a strong team of highly qualified, gifted leaders who can pull their load and a little more.

As the team is being built, someone must set values, goals, standards, philosophies, and vision which are then agreed upon by the team. The team should not all be of the same gift mix, but should have people with a variety of gifts which allow for the congregation to grow in all areas.

The Set Man as culture analyst

The Set Man studies, analyzes and seeks to understand the flow of culture.

. . . .

A team cannot be effective if its understanding of change is erroneous, incomplete, misinformed, or outdated.

. . . .

Understanding the moral, social, economical, political, and spiritual climate is important to the leader who seeks to build a church in touch with society. A leadership team cannot be effective if its understanding of change is erroneous, incomplete, misinformed, or outdated. Team members must know the difference between truth, which is unchangeable, and methods, procedures, and programs which are changeable.

The Set Man must interpret culture by studying materials, people, and expert opinions. Based on his study, he creates and implements new ideas.

George Barna's books "The Frog in the Kettle" and "The User Friendly Church" will help a leader analyze culture. [6]

The Set Man as a motivator

The Set Man motivates others to fulfill defined tasks.

. . . .

Once people know where they are
going, they will pursue vision with
a vengeance.

. . . .

He needs to know the art of motivating people.
Motivation is a key to all activities in the church.
People easily become bogged down, lose perspective,
become discouraged and side-tracked.   They need
motivation to keep going. Once people know where
they are going, they will pursue the vision with a
vengeance.

For most people motivation is not automatic. As
a matter of fact it is downright hard for most. That is
why the Set Man must be a positive motivator to staff,
to the leadership team, and to the flock.

Exhort people to start where they are, use what
they have, and do what they can.

Let us not become weary in doing good for at
the proper time we will reap a harvest if we do
not give up (Galatians 6:9).

The Set Man as servant

The Set Man serves others with proper
motivation, seeking to develop their potential.

Jesus is the model leader for every Set Man to
follow. In Luke 4:1-21 we see Jesus establishing his
leadership style by rejecting wrong leadership styles
and philosophy. He rejected the self-satisfying style of
leadership. He decided His ministry would not focus on
providing personal pleasure.

Jesus was offered rulership over all the kingdoms by the tempter. In reply, He rejected a display of His power to establish Him as a popular leader.

Jesus chose the style of a servant (See Matthew 20:20-28; Mark 10:35-44; Luke 22:24-27; Mark 9:35; Luke 9:48; John 13:14). The Set Man as servant is one of the most important distinctives a leader can develop. He must lead out of relationship, never by coercion. He must never demand obedience or submission. He should demonstrate consistent concern, love, and servanthood to all those with whom he works.

. . . .

As the Set Man moves into servant leadership, fear of people will be removed.

. . . .

The Set Man leads by support rather than by control. He should always give from himself rather than take for himself. This style of leadership develops potential in others. The servant leader allows for a loving atmosphere to permeate the team of leaders, rejecting manipulation, exploitation or domination.

A servant leader has a life full of crosses, towels and basins. He never seeks position. He seeks kingdom productivity. When a Set Man leads out of servanthood, he leads out of brokenness, not bossiness. Remember, servants are sometimes abused and insulted. They are never really appreciated to the full depth of their worth.

As the Set Man moves into servant leadership, fear of people will be removed. Fearful leaders are likely either to dictate their wishes to people or to avoid

others altogether. Let us arise with our towel, basin of
water, and a new spirit of servanthood to those around
us!

> For you I am bishop.
> But with you, I am a Christian.
> The first is an office accepted.
> The second a grace received.
> One a danger, the other safety.
> In them I am gladder by far
> to be redeemed with you
> than I am to be placed over you.
> I shall, as the commanded,
> be more completely your servant.
> —Augustine, 354-430

CHAPTER TWELVE

MINISTRY TENSIONS
AND THE SET MAN

Highlights

- A healthy church has many tensions.

- When tensions cease to exist, so does the vitality of the church.

- Truths must be carefully balanced when issues rest on opposite poles.

A healthy church has many tensions, and when tensions cease to exist, so does the vitality of the church. Life and ministry involve all kinds of people with their unique perceptions, concerns, and problems. Diversity of opinion and varying cultural and religious traditions make tension inevitable.

Tension is the "stretching of two opposite forces while searching for a proper balance." Not all tension is bad. The existence of tension is a common sign of life. We must learn to handle positive, God-given tension with wisdom, rather than try to destroy it. This is done by carefully balancing truths that rest on opposite poles of any issue or situation.

A senior pastor will face a number of different tensions as he leads the church into maturity. These tensions include:

1. The tension between emphasis on the corporate church and on the individual believer.

2. The tension in developing close friendships within the leadership team and maintaining more of a ministry working relationship with co-laborers.

3. The tension between preaching to nurture and strengthen the church, and preaching to enlarge the vision and grow the church.

4. The tension between desire to be relevant and on the cutting edge, and the need to keep doctrinal and traditional roots.

5. The tension between maintaining a faith perspective on the vision which pushes ahead and the need to rest in the Holy Spirit, allowing God to do His part.

6. The tension between ministry to all the obvious needs in the church and community, and ministering to the group of people to which God has called the church. The tension between general and focused ministry.

7. The tension between the ability to think and perceive things as the leader, and the ability to think and perceive things the way the average person in the church would.

8. The tension between leading with authority that demands respect, and dominating people with intimidation which could be perceived as manipulation.

9. The tension between discipling leaders with strong guidelines, convictions, and principles, or encouraging leaders to develop their own convictions, philosophy, and ministry techniques.

10. The tension between balancing the Word and the Spirit, sound theology and perceived fanaticism, healthy intellectualism and emotionalism. If emotionalism is out of control we should remember the warning, "If we use all the steam for the whistle on the train, there will be no steam left to move the train."

Leaders must learn to handle God-given tensions by carefully balancing the truths of God's Word. As biblical tensions are properly handled, the church will be brought closer to a place of maturity.

CHAPTER THIRTEEN

THE SET MAN'S UNIQUE STRUGGLES

Highlights

- The Set Man wrestles with who he is supposed to be, who he wants to be, and who he has to be.

- The Lord will lead people out of the church for their good.

- The battle of a carnal mind and an unsubmissive flesh.

- Be a real person, approachable.

- Sometimes relationships bring disappointment.

The Set Man has unique struggles. He wrestles continually with many opponents. At times these opponents seem to attack from every side. The leader must learn to fight well, keep his footing, maintain his perspective, and persevere through prayer.

Chryosostom, (an early church father 347-407 AD) once said, "The minister's shortcoming simply cannot be concealed. Even the most trivial ones soon become known. However trifling the offenses, these little things seem great to others, since everyone measures sin, not by the size of the offense but by the standing of the sinner."

Following are twenty-one areas in which the Set Man may find himself wrestling.

- **The Set Man wrestles with image**

The image of the minister shaped by the world around us usually is negative. The media-shaped image of the minister is quite depressing. The church-built image of the minister is one of a pious, poverty-destined, always-available doormat. The Set Man may wrestle with who he is supposed to be, who he wants to be, and who he has to be. Perhaps no other profession finds itself trapped by contrasting expectation and distorted stereotypes. Small wonder that many ministers succumb to the strong temptation to let the role prescribe and define their personalities and actions. (See II Corinthians 5:1-3; 10:10; 12:11.)

• **The Set Man wrestles with relationships.**

He is tempted not to make close friends in the church. He is tempted not to be transparent and to hide his emotions. It is so easy to get hurt! But that is part of the ministry. God's healing is part of God's mercy (II Corinthians 7:3).

Many ministers pay a heavy price for not admitting their loneliness in the ministry, and for not facing it and grappling with it honestly. They pay a price in terms of happiness and fulfillment with their self-images, and in their professional and family lives. It is hard to overestimate the importance of sharing with one another our struggles, pains, and healings. Yet it seems in the ministry that relationships are hard to develop. We have the continual pressure of others' needs upon us, a busy schedule, family, and of course church activities. What about time to develop true genuine friendships that are built for the long haul? I am privileged to have a few choice, very close friends who I can share with, be accountable to, and be real with. Loneliness happens in the ministry when there is the absence of purposeful activity and meaningful relationships.

• **The Set Man wrestles with resentment.**

When someone leaves the church it is so easy to take it personally. Remember, it is Christ's church. People do not always treat the Set Man with respect or love. He cannot take everything to heart. The Lord will lead people out of the church for their own good and sometimes for the church's good.

- **The Set Man wrestles with expectations put on him.**

It is difficult to tell whether the expectations to which we respond are primarily from others or from within ourselves. Most of us realize there are things we cannot do and things we do not know, but we do not generally let this mark of humanity show. We need to shed the burden of unrealistic expectations.

. . . .

Only we can decide what God expects of us.

. . . .

Wife, children, the staff, people, sheep, goats-- they all have ideas on how the Set Man should relate to them and on what he should do. However, only we can decide what God expects of us.

- **The Set Man wrestles with priorities.**

Like most people, pastors have priorities, a list of things we value in order of importance. But it's one thing to have the list and another thing to know how to follow it. What about family, friendships, God, health, recreation? What should be done first, today?
(II Corinthians 1:17).

- **The Set Man wrestles with guilt.**

At some point all pastors have the thought, "I'm not a good pastor. If I only would have done this, they wouldn't have gone through with the divorce. If I would have just said this. I'm not a good parent, I need to give my children more time. My body is really out of shape, I need to spend more time taking care of God's temple."

. . . .

Honesty with the congregation will release the Set Man from undue pressure to be perfect.

. . . .

• **The Set Man wrestles with flesh.**

The Set Man wrestles with the "be perfect" syndrome usually prevalent in the church. Ministers usually keep up their masks of righteousness at all cost. They are expected not to have trouble with any major carnal problems.

Of course this is not reality. We all deal with the battle of a carnal mind and an unsubmissive flesh. A modest honesty with the congregation will help educate them and release the Set Man from undue pressure to be perfect (See II Corinthians 7:1, Romans 7; Jude 24).

• **The Set Man wrestles with emotions.**

If the Set Man accepts the call to be Emmanuel, a spiritual superman, then emotions must be concealed. The pastor is expected to be tough-skinned if criticized or abused, but super sensitive if someone else is hurting. What does he do with all of these suppressed emotions? Aren't ministers supposed to cry or get emotional once in a while? (I Corinthians 2:3).

• **The Set Man wrestles with professionalism.**

To be professional as a minister is not negative in itself. We should endeavor to be excellent in our letter writing, returning of phone calls, dress, appearance, and general managerial responsibilities. But let us not cease being a real person, an approachable kind of leader. If we become too professional we may repel people instead of draw them (See II Corinthians 5:12).

• **The Set Man wrestles with the limitations of his calling.**

What are the limitations of our calling? How does one walk within that certain sphere? Time is so limited, how does one know if he has taken on too much? One person can't do everything! (II Corinthians 10:13-16). I would recommend that all leaders try to discover their spiritual gifting, talents, and aptitude as accurately as possible. The California Inventory Test was one of the most helpful tools I found in leading me to discover my strengths and weaknesses.

• **The Set Man wrestles with reality.**

In the world of ministry, we always deal with what *ought* to be. We preach with faith that all things are possible through Christ. Christ is able to break any stronghold of the devil in peoples' lives. God will answer our prayers, God is our Jehovah Jireh. Without doing harm to faith in God or the Bible, we must live with unanswered prayer, people who are struggling with bad habits they can't seem to conquer, marriages that don't work and backslidden children of wonderful Christian parents. Reality is defined by Websters

Dictionary as, "Actual being or existence of anything, truth, fact, in distinction from mere appearance."

- **The Set Man wrestles with confidence.**

Sometimes the Set Man wrestles with lack of confidence, other times too much. When should he practice humility and when should he walk in confidence of faith? (II Corinthians 3:3-6).

- **The Set Man wrestles with tiredness.**

We feel guilty when we are tired. The continual burden of the ministry wears us down. We read about John Wesley and others who got by with so little sleep, who preached four times a day and wrote all night. Who can measure up? (II Corinthians 1:8; 7:5; 2:13; Judges 8:4).

- **The Set Man wrestles with role tension.**

. . . .

Penetrating carnality and exposing lukewarmness is not readily received!

. . . .

There is role tension between pastor and prophet. The pastoral role is one of comforting and caring. During the weddings, funerals and family crisis the pastor is always welcome and respected. Move, however, into the prophet role of confronting sin in people's lives and there is a tremendous change of attitude toward the Set Man. Rather than polite respect.

you may encounter bitter criticism and hostility. No one seems to criticize the pastoral functions of baptizing or marrying, but penetrating carnality and exposing lukewarmness is not readily received!

- **The Set Man wrestles with genuine fruitfulness.**

We live in an age of fierce competition among athletes, politicians, and businesses. The minister also is affected by the competition syndrome. What are the proofs of success in the ministry? Today, the church-growth movement has raised everyone's awareness of numbers. "How many people do you have in your church?" is a question readily asked by fellow ministers as well as by people looking for a church to attend. This alone puts a tremendous amount of pressure on the ministry to be more productive. Under pressure, ministers can find their attention shifting onto external goals and away from internal fruit in lives. Achieving more goals is seen as being more fruitful, yet true fruitfulness is achieved in submission to the will of God. Is it true fruitfulness or mere human achievement? Let us keep Christ as our center and work toward the simplicity of the Christ-life as a minister leading others to experience Christ.

- **The Set Man wrestles with discouragement.**

The Set Man is always trying to encourage others, but who encourages him when he is at the end of his strength? Where are the Hurs and Aarons?
(II Corinthians 4:1, 8-10; 7:6 Exodus 17:1-5).
Discouragement will come at times to every leader. Read the Scriptures and you encounter leader

after leader who had seasons of discouragement. Jonah, Elijah, Jeremiah, David, Peter, Paul, and John Mark left the ministry for a time because of discouragement. William Carey, the late, great missionary to India was asked, "What is the secret to your success?", He replied, "I can plod." This is the ability to keep on keeping on. He was known as the man who wouldn't give in to any pressure or opposition. No matter how great the obstacle, he expected great things and attempted great things for God. Don't let discouragement keep you from attempting great things for God. Remember, today's mighty oak is yesterday's little nut that held its ground.

- **The Set Man wrestles with judging others.**

If someone leaves our church we may think it is because they can't handle the flow of God in the place. We tend to think, "I am right, they are wrong." (II Corinthians 5:16).

- **The Set Man wrestles with unanswered prayers.**

It makes me irritable to pray so much and have so little happen. Sometimes I don't understand the ministry of prayer.

For eleven years my wife was barren. I prayed and prayed but nothing happened. During a meeting at another church the Lord told me to pray for the barren women in the church. My response was, "You've got to be kidding!" I finally had an altar call for those who were barren and several women responded. I prayed for each one. A year later some of the ones prayed for had babies. We had adopted two lovely daughters, but my wife was still barren! When

Sharon did became pregnant many years later, I didn't believe her when she told me!

Sometimes unanswered prayer is answered prayer on God's timetable!

•   **The Set Man wrestles with the relentless march of time.**

Time keeps going. We run out of time and we keep getting older. (See Ecclesiastes 3:1-11).

Every person has an equal amount of time, 168 hours each week. One of the most significant measures of a person's spiritual commitment is what he does with his discretionary or leisure time. We should not feel guilty when we use leisure time wisely by recreating, reading a book or some chosen hobby. But time wasters must be dealt with harshly or they may ruin our spiritual potential in God.

The following chart from R. Alec McKenzie, *The Time Trap*, puts time wasters into four groups for those in top management.

GROUP A

Unclear Objectives
Poor Information
Postponed decisions
Procrastination
Lack of information
Lack of feedback
Routine work
Too much reading
Interruptions
Telephone
No time planning
Meetings
Beautiful secretaries
Lack of competent personnel
Lack of delegation
Visitors
Training new staff
lack of priorities
Management by crises

GROUP C

Trash mail Socializing
Unnecessary meetings
Lack of concentration
Lack of managerial tools
Peer demands on time
Incompetent subordinates
Coffee breaks
Crises management
Unintelligible communications
Procrastination
Lack of clerical staff
Poor physical fitness
Red tape
Pet project
Lack of priorities

GROUP B

Scheduled meetings
Unscheduled meetings
Lack of priorities
Failure to delegate
Interruptions
Unavailability of people
Junk mail
Lack of planning
Outside (civic) demands
Poor filing system
Fatigue
Procrastination
Telephone
Questionnaires
Lack of procedure for routine matters

GROUP D

Attempting too much at once
Lack of delegation
Talking too much
Inconsistent actions
No priorities
Span of control
Usurped authority
Can't say no
Lack of planning
Snap decision
Procrastination
Low morale
Mistakes
Disorganized secretaries
Poor communication
Overoptimism
Responsibility without authority

- **The Set Man wrestles with disappointments.**

The Set Man hears many hollow promises of commitment and relationship only to be disappointed time after time. It hurts to be dropped relationally, so it is much easier to avoid risking the injury that comes when you depend on others. But the ministry is a place to love, trust, and believe in people and in God.

- **The Set Man wrestles with his own lack of Christlikeness.**

We ask ourselves "Why am I not more like Jesus? This is my profession! I read the Bible, I pray more than most people, yet I see such a lack of Christlikeness."

THE WINNER'S CREED

People are unreasonable, illogical and self-centered-- LOVE THEM ANYWAY.

If you do good, people will accuse you of being selfish and having an ulterior motive--DO GOOD ANYWAY.

If you are successful, you will win false friends and true enemies--SUCCEED ANYWAY.

Honesty and frankness make you vulnerable--BE HONEST AND FRANK ANYWAY.

The good you do today will be forgotten tomorrow--DO GOOD ANYWAY.

The biggest people with the biggest ideas can be shot down by the smallest people with the smallest minds--THINK BIG ANYWAY.

People favor underdogs, but follow top dogs--FIGHT FOR SOME UNDERDOGS ANYWAY.

What you spend building for years may be destroyed overnight--BUILD ANYWAY.

Give the world the best you have and you'll always get kicked in the teeth--GIVE THE WORLD THE BEST YOU'VE GOT ANYWAY.

When you were born, you cried and the world rejoiced. Let the rest of your life be in such a fashion so that when you die, the world cries and you rejoice.

—Author Unknown

CHAPTER FOURTEEN

RELEASING RESOURCES FOR THE VISION

Highlights

- To shrink back from preaching on finances is to fail at bringing the vision to fulfillment.

- The senior pastor sets the attitude toward giving.

- Satan's lie: God takes more than He gives.

- When God's people are taught to order their finances according to the Word of God, blessing follows.

The fulfillment of every local church dream has three parts: The man, the mission, and the money. A simple diagram taken from the life of Moses illustrates the threefold cord.

Receives the Vision
Mission
Exodus 24: 9-18

The Man

Exodus 24: 1-7

The Need of
Money

Exodus 25: 1-9
Exodus 35: 4-9
Exodus 35: 20-26
Exodus 36: 3-7

Moses is called to the top of the mountain to receive his mission. He must come down the mountain to the reality of needed resources!

Moses was the man God called to the top of the mountain to receive God's vision for the people--a divinely ordered tabernacle for worship. To bring the vision into reality tangible things were needed--gold, silver and precious stones. Or as we would say today, money.

Every Set Man must deal successfully with the challenge money presents. Some pastors have a vision larger than their finances. Some pastors have great faith for spiritual dreams and visions but struggle when it comes to financing the vision.

To shrink back from boldly preaching on finances is to fail at bringing the vision to fulfillment. Paul stated in Acts 20:27,31 that he did not shrink back but boldly spoke the whole counsel of God. To fail to declare the whole revelation of finance to your church will rob it of divine blessing and cause it to fall short of the divine vision. We must preach giving of finance with faith and a proper doctrinal balance.

One of every seven verses in the New Testament speaks of money. A recent magazine article stated that people spend fifty percent of their time thinking about money--how to get it, spend it, and use it. We as leaders must give a biblical perspective on money to those we are responsible for. Every person has a financial responsibility before God and the local church to the God- ordained vision.

· ·

Without money the vision will stay on the drawing board, unfulfilled and unprofitable.

· ·

The Set Man will set the attitude toward giving in the church. If the pastor and leadership team display a liberal, faith-filled, joyful attitude toward giving, then the church will also.

> There is one who scatters, yet increases more; and there is one who withholds more than is right, but it leads to poverty (Proverbs 11:24).

Satan is a blatant liar. He tries to put a guilt trip on pastors concerning money. He tries to question motives and condemn leaders. Sure there are leaders who misuse money and the people from whom they get money. God will always be the judge of men's hearts and ministries.

Most leaders do not misuse people or money, but the devil would like to keep elders in a place of fear and doubt so the vision will stay on the drawing board, unfulfilled and unprofitable.

We, as God's servants, must expose Satan's blatant lies. Satan's lie is that God will take more than He will give. God is not a miserly penny pincher. He is Lord over all the wealth of the universe. He is the Lord of abundance. He is not in the depriving business, but in the blessing business.

God wants to trust His leaders with wealth and abundance. As righteous leaders with integrity we never need to stoop down to coercion or manipulation of God's people. We want to stimulate and motivate God's people but we must do it God's way. We must lift up the Word of God as the right way of thinking about money.

> Honor the Lord with your possessions, and with the firstfruits of all your increase; So your barns

will be filled with plenty, and your vats will overflow with new wine (Proverbs 3:9-10).

Give, and it will be given to you: good measure, pressed down, shaken together, and running over will be put into your bosom. For with the same measure that you use, it will be measured back to you (Luke 6:38).

And you shall remember the Lord your God, for it is He who gives you power to get wealth, that He may establish His covenant which He swore to your fathers, as it is this day (Deuteronomy 8:18).

And all these blessings shall come upon you and overtake you, because you obey the voice of the Lord your God (Deuteronomy 28:2).

Thus says the Lord, your Redeemer, the Holy One of Israel: "I am the Lord your God, Who teaches you to profit, Who leads you by the way you should go" (Isaiah 48:17).

The Set Man of the church must warn the people concerning the misuse of money.

Do not trust in oppression, Nor vainly hope in robbery; If riches increase, Do not set your heart on them (Psalm 62;10).

But those who desire to be rich fall into temptation and a snare, and into many foolish and harmful lusts which drown men in destruction and perdition. For the love of money is a root of

all kinds of evil, for which some have strayed
from the faith in their greediness, and pierced
themselves through with many sorrows
(I Timothy 6:9-10).

Billy Graham once said, "If a man gets his attitude toward money straight, it will help straighten out
almost every other area of his life."

As leaders we must teach the people of God to
abandon selfish ambitions to achieve wealth and prosperity. People must develop a kingdom philosophy, a
kingdom world view. He who lays up treasures for
himself is not rich toward God (Luke 12:15-20).

· ·

The rich young ruler backed away
from discipleship because Jesus
would have assumed lordship over
his finances.

· ·

The obvious unabashed goal of many North
American Christians is to hoard wealth so that retire-
ment will be bliss. There is nothing wrong with future
financial planning, but we must make sure the kingdom
of God receives abundantly from our hand now. When
people of God are taught to order their financial lives
according to the Word of God, blessing follows. We
must learn to trust God's ability to meet abundantly all
our material needs. As a leader, I must be confident in
God's Word and bold in faith to proclaim it. I can then
teach the people to give in faith and put all that they
have at His disposal.

Jesus is the Lord over our finances. To acknowledge Jesus as Savior is commitment based on grace, or
what He can do for us. To acknowledge Him as Lord
is commitment based on obedience, or what we can do
for Him (Matthew 19:16-22; Luke 6:46).

. . . .

Money is a trust from God, and
must be earned and managed
according to biblical principles.

. . . .

The rich young ruler backed away from discipleship because Jesus would have assumed lordship over
his finances. Any concept we teach concerning the lordship of Christ which ignores or slights Christ's right to
totally control people's material possessions is superficial and inadequate. Money is a trust from God and
must be earned and managed according to scriptural
principles.

God is looking for men and women who will
obey His principles of finance and demonstrate to a
skeptical unbelieving world that He lives and He is a
rewarder of those who diligently seek Him.

The tithe is the foundation for financial blessing
in the life of the believer and in the local church.
Giving must begin with the tithe, and the Set Man must
teach the church the principle of tithing.

- **The tithe is the first of our wages and the first
  of our increase.**

And now, behold, I have brought the firstfruits
of the land which you, O Lord, have given me.

Then you shall set it before the Lord your God, and worship before the Lord your God...When you have finished laying aside all the tithe of your increase in the third year, which is the year of tithing, then you shall give it to the Levite, the stranger, the fatherless, and the widow, so that they may eat within your gates and be filled (Deuteronomy 26:10,12).

See also Proverbs 3:9-10.

• **The tithe acknowledges all we have has come from the goodness of God.**

Beware lest you forget the Lord your God by not keeping His commandments and His ordinances and His statutes which I am commanding you today...But you shall remember the Lord your God, for it is He who is giving you power to make wealth, that He may confirm His covenant which He swore to your fathers, as it is this day (Deuteronomy 8:11,18).

See also Deuteronomy 26:10.

• **The tithe is to be given with an attitude of worship.**

Mary therefore took a pound of very costly perfume of pure nard, and anointed the feet of Jesus, and wiped His feet with her hair; and the house was filled with the fragrance of the perfume (John 12:3).

See also II Corinthians 9:7; Deuteronomy 26:12

- **The tithe is to be given from our increase.**

  When you have finished laying aside all the tithe of your increase in the third year, which is the year of tithing, and have given it to the Levite, the stranger, the fatherless, and the widow, so that they may eat within your gates and be filled (Deuteronomy 26:12).

- **The tithe is the sacred portion we set aside as the Lord's. It is holy.**

  Then you shall say before the Lord your God: "I have removed the holy tithe from my house, and also have given them to the Levite, the stranger, the fatherless, and the widow, according to all Your commandments which You have commanded me; I have not transgressed Your commandments, nor have I forgotten them" (Deuteronomy 26:13).

  See also Leviticus 27:26-33.

- **The tithe is not to be used for personal needs.**

  I have not eaten any of it when in mourning, nor have I removed any of it for any unclean use, nor given any of it for the dead (Deuteronomy 26:14).

  See also Leviticus 27:30.

• **The tithe is to be given as an act of spiritual obedience.**

I have not eaten any of it ... I have obeyed the voice of the Lord my God, and have done according to all that You have commanded me (Deuteronomy 26:14).

• **The tithe is the basis to receive God's covenantal blessings or covenantal cursings.**

Look down from Your holy habitation, from heaven, and bless Your people Israel and the land which You have given us, just as You swore to our fathers, "a land flowing with milk and honey,"...and that He will set you high above all nations which He has made, in praise, in name, and in honor, and that you may be a holy people to the Lord your God, just as He has spoken (Deuteronomy 26:15,19).

See also Malachi 3:8.

• **The tithe is the provision for releasing ministry in the local church.**

I also realized that the portions for the Levites had not been given them; for each of the Levites and the singers who did the work had gone back to his field. So I contended with the rulers, and said, "Why is the house of God forsaken?" And I gathered them together and set them in their place. Then all Judah brought the tithe of the grain and the new wine and the oil to the store-house (Nehemiah 13:10-12).

See also I Corinthians 9:9; Acts 28:10

- **The blessings of the tithe are in the New Testament as well as the Old Testament.**

    Woe to you, scribes and Pharisees, hypocrites! For you pay tithe of mint and anise and cumin, and have neglected the weightier matters of the law: justice and mercy and faith. These you ought to have done, without leaving the others undone (Matthew 23:23).

    There is one who scatters, yet increases more; and there is one who withholds more than is right, but it leads to poverty. The generous soul will be made rich, and he who waters will also be watered himself. The people will curse him who withholds grain, but blessing will be on the head of him who sells it (Proverbs 11:24-26).

    See also Matthew 6:1; I Corinthians 16:1-2

Together, tithes and offerings make up a balanced giving program. In our church, we look for all of our members--one hundred percent of them--to tithe. Then, to carry out God's plan for our church, the eldership establishes a wise budget.

CHAPTER FIFTEEN

MINISTRY TEMPTATION AND THE SET MAN

Highlights

- A Set Man may be excellent in his message but bring reproach to Christ and His church because of his conduct and methods.

- The Set Man must continually be on guard against spiritual dry rot.

- The temptations of spiritual decay are numerous and devious.

To promote the highest end of the ministry, the servant of God must begin with himself. Plato once said, "An unexamined life is not worth living." Leaders, especially the Set Man, must continually examine their lives before God and His Word.

> Therefore take heed to yourselves and to all the flock, among which the Holy Spirit has made you overseers, to shepherd the church of God which He purchased with His own blood (Acts 20:28).

See also I Corinthians 9:26-27; Acts 26:16.

· ·

The temptations of spiritual decay
are numerous and devious.

· ·

Along with his message and his methods, the messenger himself is important. A Set Man can bring an excellent message but bring a reproach on Christ and His church with his conduct and methods.

The Set Man must continually be on guard against spiritual dry rot. Dry rot is a disease which destroys fibers in wood, eventually reducing boards and entire trees to a mass of dry dust.

Without spiritual seasoning or Holy Ghost preserving, the servant of God is in danger of spiritual decay. It is not always noticeable. Spiritual dry rot may take place in every level of a leader's life and ministry.

The temptations toward spiritual decay are numerous and devious. We must continually be on guard.

· ·

The longer one is in the ministry the more receptive one becomes to certain hidden temptations.

· ·

Gregory the Great once said, "He who is required by the necessity of his position to speak the highest things is compelled by the same necessity to exemplify the highest things." We are called to a high calling. We stand yet in a dangerous place.

Martin Luther said, "Prayer, meditation, and temptation make a minister." The longer one is in the ministry the more receptive one may become to certain hidden temptations. Let us consider a few of the ones all Set Man leaders will encounter sooner or later.

1.   The temptation to become administrator of things more than serving people out of love and calling.

2.   The temptation to become mechanical and robotic with the things of God--becoming a professional minister. Becoming more interested in the letter of correct theology than with ministering to people.

3.   The temptation to coast with one's own spiritual maturity, thinking that leadership is equal to maturity. We may become blinded by our own success and ministry accomplishments.

4.   The temptation to seek material security as the basis for our joy and happiness.

5.   The temptation to become hardened and distrustful toward people because of disappointments and disillusionment. All Asia turn against Paul, yet he ended his last epistle with a statement of love and trust for people.

6.   The temptation to find satisfaction in the failure of another leader. This usually is motivated by an ungodly jealousy. Jealousy amplifies our human nature and lets loose the hell within.

7.   The temptation to measure ministry success by numbers, buildings and budgets instead of the spiritual quality and maturity of the people.

8.   The temptation to react against new truth because of who proclaims the truth.

9.   The temptation to excuse little sins, habits and shortcomings because of our stress and sacrificial lifestyle.

10.   The temptation to use people for personal gain, ministry status, or goal accomplishment.

11.   The temptation to function in ministry out of learned habits and legal principles, instead of living out the life of Christ that comes only by abiding in Christ. In our hurried daily lives, we are in danger of losing our souls and the secret known by Paul (Philippians 1:21).

> There is an altar in men, a deep majestic place
> where the soul transcends with its God and life
> is cleansed and kindled with an unearthly flame.
> It is the altar that makes the man.
>
> --E.M. Bounds

12.   The temptation to allow the things of God to become too familiar so as to become presumptuous about sacred things. (See I Samuel 3:12-14)

13.   The temptation to replace the precious with the lesser or second best, to find a less expensive substitute. In I Kings 14:26 the leaders took away the shields of gold and replaced them with shields of brass. Compared to gold, brass is cheap. A casual glance might show the appearance to be the same, but the substance is changed. Brass may be of utility to some, but it is a sign of lesser value, a debasing of the highest ideal, a cheap substitute for the best.

I'm sure we all identify with many of these temptations both out of knowledge and experience. The ministry was never intended to provide us with a safe place or a comfortable living. It is the fellowship of his sufferings on the cross we are called to. These temptations can be overcome successfully by abiding in the living Christ and eating the living Word of God. Do not lose heart if you have yielded to some of those temptations in the past, its a new day, a day of victory.

> What lies behind us and what lies before us
> are tiny matters compared to what lies within us.
>
> --Oliver Wendell Holmes

CHAPTER SIXTEEN

PRINCIPLES AND THE SET MAN

Highlights

- Principles sustain the church; emotions can not.

- Principles never change like styles and trends.

- The Set Man weak in biblical principles becomes prey to trends and fads.

- The stability of the church will be determined by the Set Man's ability to establish strong principles.

The church Christ is building will withstand the attack of the enemy. The winds, rains and floods will not move the true church from its solid rock foundation. The house built on a right foundation in Matthew 7:24-27 can represent a church built on right principles. Principles sustain a church when emotions or exciting things can not.

Every church wants to be exciting and to stay exciting, but life does not sustain this ideal. Every church has up times and down times, times of revival and times of dryness.

When a Set Man builds the church on principles, seasons do not hinder progress. People with principles obey the written Word of God with or without excited emotions. A Set Man who wants to be on the cutting edge might use hype to keep people involved when emotions are down and the cloud of excitement has lifted, but principles guarantee longevity.

The word *principle* comes from the word prince or first, leader. It can signify precepts, respected methods of operation or guidelines which shape an organization. A principle is a guiding force, a comprehensive and fundamental law, doctrine, or assumption.

. . . .

Methods change from one generation to another, but principles never change.

. . . .

A trend is a current style or preference--something temporary. We can never build on temporary, passing whims of human nature. Styles and trends change constantly with the culture. Principles, however, never change. Principles are built on the unchangeable Word of God. Methods change from time to time and from one generation to another; but principles never change. A method, technique or process of doing something will change from one style of leader to another, but the principles used should remain the same.

God's eternal principles:

• Are based on the eternal values as seen in the Word of God.

• Are an extension of God's character as applied in any circumstance at any time.

• Are derived from biblical history and basic theology as presented in both the Old and New Testament.

• Are usually evident within certain biblical models such as the tabernacle of Moses, the Levitical priesthood, the conquest of Canaan, the discipline of the twelve, etc.

• Must become convictions. These convictions must conquer us and become our value system for living.

We must discern the difference between principles and methods. A principle is an extension of biblical truth. Truth does not change. A method is an extension of personality, style, culture, spiritual genes. A method is the way to apply the truth, but it is not the truth. Following is an illustration of the difference.

Principles   Methods

As principles pass through the grid of methodology, they may be weakened, strengthened, obscured, changed, or even forgotten. We must maintain the integrity of truth, yet we must use methods that are effective and easy to embrace culturally. At the same time we must be careful not to compromise truth in the name of relevancy, becoming so overly interested in communicating to our present culture that we end up making a gospel of communication or relevancy.

The Set Man must continually evaluate and examine himself to make sure he does not compromise godly principles because of a passion for success or quick growth. Methods can become like a barren woman, always unsatisfied. Beware of trying to make methods better, more attractive, and more tolerable to a humanistic, narcissistic, antinomian culture.

. . . .

A church which lacks a solid foundation of basic principles has no secure way to evaluate spiritual fads.

. . . .

The Set Man who is weak in biblical principles will become prey to trends and spiritual fads. Truth is sought and applied on many levels according to the maturity level of the church. Therefore, what might seem trendy for one might be truth for another. A church which lacks the solid foundation of the basic principles has no secure way to evaluate spiritual fads and many other problems.

The Set Man is responsible to build on the rock-solid biblical principles that have been tried and proven by the Word of God. The Set Man should continually ask himself these questions:

• Am I responding to truth or trend?

• Am I responding to personality or personal convictions?

• Am I responding for spiritual reasons or selfish reasons?

• Am I responding cautiously or hastily?

(See Psalm 85:11, 86:11, 117:2; Proverbs 23:23, 25:8, 14:29, 29:20.)

The Set Man is the helmsman. Wherever he turns the wheel the whole church goes. The Set Man is responsible to make sure he is on the right biblical track before he fires up his engine and goes full steam ahead, possibly right off a cliff!

. . . .

Leadership that builds on principles rather than hype, personality, or fads is an endangered species.

. . . .

Three ingredients move the church forward: basic Bible doctrines, biblical principles, and methods. Picture a wheel, with a hub, spokes, and the rim.

The hub represents the theological, unchangeable, basic doctrines of the Bible which become the foundation for the church's mission statements, purpose, vision, and destiny, out of which all strategies are built.

The spokes represent the unchangeable principles which become the expressions of truth in principle statements, precepts, concepts, and philosophy.

The rim represents the changeable styles, procedures and ideas for applying and communicating truth to the present times and culture. It represents the methods whereby truth is applied.

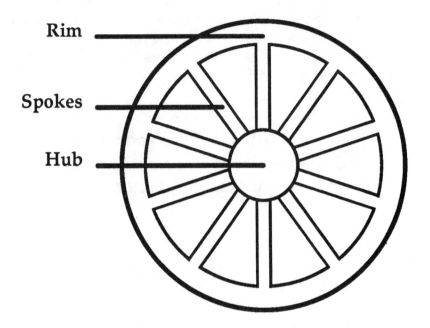

Rim

Spokes

Hub

The Set Man is responsible to understand the basic doctrine of the Word of God. Theology, if neglected, will make it impossible to establish strong principles. The stability of the local church will be determined by the ability of the Set Man to establish strong principles and sustain them in trendy times.

Leadership that builds on principles rather than hype, personality or fads, is truly an endangered species. Every Set Man needs to develop a theological motif--an overall emphasis that is spoken or unspoken but is the shaping invisible force behind everything he does. Here are fifteen principles needed to build churches that last:

1. The Dynamic Hub

Approach every consideration in this way: work from the whole to the part, and from the part back to the whole. Remember that the body corporate exists to express the life of God in community, as well as to release and benefit individual believers. Remember each believer exists to express the life of God, as well as to benefit the corporate good.

The Corporate
Colossians 1: 24-28
Ephesians 2: 20-22

The Individual
Colossians 1: 24-28
I Corinthians 6: 19-20

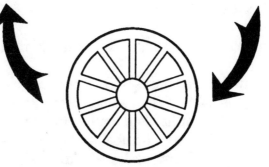

HUB
Eternal Purpose
of God
Ephesians 5: 25-31
I Corinthians 12: 12-30
Ephesians 4:12-16
Matthew 16: 16-18

2. The Objective Rules the Subjective

Subjectivity without biblical truth is dangerous because its roots may be in ourselves, our experiences, moods, gifting, or spiritual biases. Subjectivity can be confused with prophetic feelings or inner voices of the inner man, when in reality it is simply a strong opinion, view, or desire. We must allow the Word of God to have preeminence in all things. Subjective thoughts and ideas cannot be allowed to prevail.

3.   The Clear Interprets the Obscure

The Bible has a very simple, forthright redemptive message. When this message is confused by a teacher or preacher using obscure types, shadows, or metaphors to establish an obscure plan of God, it is violating Christ's model. Christ preached a clear message from clear biblical passages in establishing His mission, vision and strategy.

4.   The Major Emphasis Rules the Minor

The major emphases of Scripture are easily found throughout the Bible. When a leader begins to slip away from the major emphasized truths to focus on minor truths, he runs the risk of imbalance and possible spiritual shipwreck. The apostles' doctrine should be the foundation for pastoral preaching and local church foundations.

5.   Proven Basics Come Before Unproven Success Ideas

Most aggressive leaders desire to be innovative and on the cutting edge. Consequently, the willingness to take risks and explore new truths and new methods may become a snare to the leader.

. . . .

Better to build slowly with proven principles of God's Word than risk it all in the name of innovation.

. . . .

All unproven success ideas should be taken with a grain of salt. It is better to build slowly with the proven principles of God's Word and proven church patterns than to risk it all in the name of innovation. We need to commit ourselves to God's theological non-negotiables:

- The glory of God is the chief end of all men and women.

- The preaching of the Gospel is the preaching of the kingdom.

- The Scriptures are the only normative authority for believers.

- Sin, salvation, and eternal death are eschatological realities.

- God desires all to be saved from sin and eternal death.

- God is the supreme Ruler over His church, His servants. Everything is done in submission to Him.

6.   The Principle of the Cross

The Cross is the hermeneutical filter by which all truths from Genesis to Revelation must pass through. If you cannot get your truth through the Cross then you must let it go. What the Cross cancels or fulfills must be handled in the same fashion.

> Therefore we also, since we are surrounded by so great a cloud of witnesses, let us lay aside every weight, and the sin which so easily ensnares us, and let us run with endurance the race that is set before us, looking unto Jesus, the author and finisher of our faith, who for the joy that was set before Him endured the cross, despising the shame, and has sat down at the right hand of the throne of God (Hebrews 12:1-2).

> And being found in appearance as a man, He humbled Himself and became obedient to the point of death, even the death of the cross (Philippians 2:8).

. . . .

The whole Bible looks to and from the Cross with an ultimate victory in mind.

. . . .

> And by Him to reconcile all things to Himself, by Him, whether things on earth or things in heaven, having made peace through the blood of His cross. And you, who once were alienated and enemies in your mind by wicked works, yet

now He has reconciled In the body of His flesh through death, to present you holy, and blameless, and irreproachable in His sight (Colossians 1:20-22).

The French theologian, Calvin, once said, "For in the Cross of Christ, as in a splendid theater, the incomparable goodness of God is set before the whole world. The glory of God shines indeed on all creatures on high and below, but never more brightly than in the Cross." The whole Bible looks to and from the Cross with an ultimate victory in mind. We might endure our crosses more joyfully if we could perceive correctly the crown awaiting us.

Finally, there is laid up for me the crown of righteousness, which the Lord, the righteous Judge, will give to me on that Day, and not to me only but also to all who have loved His appearing (II Timothy 4:8).

The Bible derives its full meaning from the Cross. To leave the Cross out would be like taking the sun out of the sky or the heart with its arterial system out of the body. To understand the Cross and all its redemptive ramifications is to understand real authentic Christianity.

Any leader who violates the clear message of the Cross violates not just a part, but the whole. As we build Christ's church, let us keep the Cross as central. Count Zinzandorf owed much of his spiritual fervor to a picture of the crucifixion with the simple inscription at the bottom, "All this for thee, how much for me."

The Cross of Christ is the key that unlocks true spiritual blessings for the church. The message of the

Cross must be taught dearly, continually, and passionately. Christ's Cross is the fountainhead of life. This is the message of hope for all nations.

Sacrifice, surrender, and total consecration are a few of the simple but strong truths of the Cross. The principles of suffering, severance, separation, shame and glory are also present in the Cross. As we build strong Christian lives and strong churches, let us build on the Cross.

The resurrection life of God could only be released in the death of Christ on the Cross. Giving up life opens a new way of living, life in the supernatural! The Cross message helps us establish a perspective for life where self with all its rights and demands are truly on the Cross and the Lord Jesus is the center of existence.

> But God forbid that I should glory except in the cross of our Lord Jesus Christ, by whom the world has been crucified to me, and I to the world (Galatians 6:14).

> Most assuredly, I say to you, unless a grain of wheat falls into the ground and dies, it remains alone; but if it dies, it produces much grain (John 12:24).

7.   The Team Principle

When we understand the nature of God, His plan and purpose, we will see the team principle more clearly. God is triune. The Father works with the Son, the Son with the Holy Spirit, the Holy Spirit with the Word of God. Jesus worked with the twelve, and the twelve worked with the seventy.

. . . .

To work as a team is to work with
the blessing and wisdom of God.

. . . .

The team principle is seen throughout the Scriptures. Anytime we violate this principle we violate a principle in the Word of God. Pride would like to elevate one person above another, but the kingdom of God is established on humility, honoring one another. To work as a team is to work with the blessing and wisdom of God.

8.   The Biblical Vision Mandate

The vision of the local pastor and the leadership team must comprehend the scope of God's plan and purpose. A clear biblical vision should have at least four main elements:

•   *The kingdom of God is the mission.* Christ's objective was nothing less than the absolute eternal rule of God in the heavens, earth, human heart, and in the church. Mature Christians are to take the rule of Christ into the home, work place, classroom, and all facets of business. When people catch a kingdom vision they will become excited, thinking, "We are taking the rule of Christ to the world!" kingdom vision produces kingdom faith, kingdom thinkers.

•   *The cross and resurrection of Christ are the source of kingdom vision,* because through them come the many supernatural resources needed to accomplish God's vision.

• *The church is the vehicle for the kingdom to be established.* The church exists to fulfill God's will; its mission is to promote the kingdom of God. When pastors and leaders gain a kingdom mindset, they will motivate people to serve and sacrifice.

• *The Second Coming is the motive that keeps the vision sure.* The truth of Jesus' coming brings with it the possibility of rewards and the reality of accountability.

Other areas such as authority, holiness, the Holy Spirit, commitment and serving, the presence of God, and unity of leadership are also principles in the Word of God. The wise Set Man will search out God's principles in all these areas to lay a solid foundation for the church.

CHAPTER SEVENTEEN

PRAYER AND THE SET MAN

Highlights

- A movement of God will last as long as the spirit of prayer that inspired it.

- Only Prayer can change a stagnant church into a zealous, on-fire church.

- Pre-service prayer helps the church dig out its spiritual ears to hear the Word of God.

- Corporate prayer prepares people to enter into worship.

- Prayer must affect the corporate life as well as the personal devotional life of every believer in the church.

All leaders must decide where they will look for their strength, their ideas, and their reason for living. The leader's prayer life will promote a praying spirit in the church. Yongi Cho, the pastor of the world's largest church in Seoul, Korea states the problem, "Americans will give their money, sing songs, build buildings and preach, but they will not pray." John Wesley said, "God will do nothing on earth except in answer to believing prayer."

> Pray at all times--on every occasion in every season--in the Spirit, with all manner of prayer and entreaty. To that end keep alert and watch with strong purpose and perseverance, interceding in behalf of all the saints (Ephesians 6:18 AMPLIFIED).

Jack Hayford's Book, *Prayer--Invading the Impossible*, defines powerful praying. He says, "Prayer is essentially a partnership of the redeemed child of God working hard with God toward the realization of His redemptive purposes on earth."[7]

The principle of prayer is absolutely essential to moving in the redemptive purpose of God. Praying saints, praying churches, and praying leaders are God's agents for carrying on His saving and providential work on earth. If these agents neglect the discipline of prayer, then God's work will fail. Praying leaders and praying churches are a sign of spiritual life and spiritual prosperity.

A movement of God will last as long as the spirit of prayer that inspired it. If we in this age of gross darkness wish to build effective, society-changing churches, we must build with the prayer principle. It begins with praying leaders!

Mary Queen of Scots once said, "I fear John Knox's prayers more than an army of 10,000 men." Prayer in the church is the only hope of a bona fide moving of the Holy Spirit in power and purity.

Prayer puts God's work in His hands and keeps it there. Prayer is the divinely appointed means by which man comes into direct connection with God. Prayer is the only means to change a stagnant church into a zealous, on-fire church.

> Who has heard such a thing? Who has seen such things? Shall the earth be made to give birth in one day? Or shall a nation be born at once? For as soon as Zion travailed, she gave birth to her children (Isaiah 66:8).

Prayer must effect the personal devotional life of every believer in the church as well as the corporate life of the church.

Corporate prayer is the praying together of all saints in one accord, lifting their voices together.

> Even them I will bring to My holy mountain, and make them joyful in My house of prayer. Their burnt offerings and their sacrifices will be accepted on My altar; for My house shall be called a house of prayer for all nations (Isaiah 56:7).

. . . .

Pre-service prayer is a key to spiritual life, flow, and anointing.

. . . .

Then another angel, having a golden censer, came and stood at the altar. And he was given much incense, that he should offer it with the prayers of all the saints upon the golden altar which was before the throne. And the smoke of the incense, with the prayers of the saints, ascended before God from the angel's hand (Revelation 8:3-4).

Then they returned to Jerusalem from the Mount called Olivet, which is near Jerusalem, a Sabbath day's journey. And when they had entered, they went up into the upper room where they were staying: Peter, James, John, and Andrew; Philip and Thomas; Bartholomew and Matthew; James the son of Alphaeus and Simon the Zealot; and Judas the son of James. These all continued with one accord in prayer and supplication, with the women and Mary the mother of Jesus, and with His brothers (Acts 1:12-14).

Now when the day of Pentecost had fully come, they were all with one accord in one place. And suddenly there came a sound from heaven, as of a rushing mighty wind, and it filled the whole house where they were sitting. Then there appeared to them divided tongues, as of fire, and one sat upon each of them. And they were all filled with the Holy Spirit and began to speak with other tongues, as the Spirit gave them utterance (Acts 2:1-4).

So when they heard that, they raised their voice to God with one accord and said: "Lord, You are God, who made heaven and earth and the sea, and all that is in them, who by the mouth of Your servant David have said: 'Why did the nations rage, and the people plot vain things? The kings of the earth took their stand, and the rulers were gathered together against the Lord and against His Christ.' For truly against Your holy Servant Jesus, whom You anointed, both Herod and Pontius Pilate, with the Gentiles and the people of Israel, were gathered together to do whatever Your hand and Your purpose determined before to be done. Now, Lord, look on their threats, and grant to Your servants that with all boldness they may speak Your word, by stretching out Your hand to heal, and that signs and wonders may be done through the name of Your holy Servant Jesus." And when they had prayed, the place where they were assembled together was shaken; and they were all filled with the Holy Spirit, and they spoke the word of God with boldness (Acts 4:24-31).

If one can put a thousand to flight and two ten thousand, can you imagine hundreds of thousands of saints praying in unified prayer? The power is beyond comprehension! (See Psalm 141:1-2; Psalm 133:1-3; Luke 1:9-11; Matthew 18:19-20.)

. . . .

We must break the bondage of
silence in our corporate prayer
times.

. . . .

Corporate prayer can also be one person leading
with a specific goal in mind with congregational agreement and verbal participation. In Yongi Cho's book,
Prayer--Key to Revival, he describes the prayer in his
church: "One of the most important ministries of the
Full Gospel Central Church is the prayer in unison we
have during every service. We always open our services with everyone present praying together at the same
time. When we pray, we pray with determination and
assurance. When I hear the church pray it sounds like
a forceful roar of a mighty waterfall."[8]
Pre-service prayer, a one-half hour or one hour
prayer time before every service, or a period of intense
unified prayer at the beginning of each service is a key
to spiritual life, flow, and anointing. We must break the
bondage of silence in our corporate prayer times. In the
Scriptures silence usually speaks of death.

When I kept silent, my bones grew old through
my groaning all the day long (Psalm 32:3).

Unless the Lord had been my help, my soul
would soon have settled in silence (Psalm 94:17).

The dead do not praise the Lord, nor any who go
down into silence (Psalm 115:17).

He will guard the feet of His saints, but the wicked shall be silent in darkness. For by strength no man shall prevail (I Samuel 2:9).

In corporate prayer we are to lift our voices with faith and power. The Bible has a great deal to say about our voice in prayer and praise. *Lift, say, cry aloud* and *loud voice* are all words used in the Scriptures to describe prayer. (See Isaiah 37:4; 40:9; 42:11; 52:8; 58:1; Exodus 19:8; Psalm 30:12; 150:5; II Chronicles 15:14; 20:19; 30:21; Matthew 27:46; Luke 17:15; 19:37.)

. . . .

When we say amen we express our participation in the shared words of faith prayers.

. . . .

Another great Bible word that should be heard in our praying is a loud *amen!* Saying amen together during prayer identifies the people with the words being prayed, confirming what has been said as true and binding. Amen is the proper response of a congregation to endorse prayers. When we say amen we express our own participation in and our commitment to the shared words of faith prayers. Amen indicates firmness, dependability, certainty and truth.

Charles Finney, the 18th Century revivalist said, "There can be no revival when Mr. Amen and Mr. Wet Eyes are not found in the audience."

The Set Man should establish a strong prayer time during or before the service. Corporate prayer is one of Christ's principles practiced in the book of Acts with the first church, and it has continued to be a key throughout the ages.

• Corporate prayer is the army of God moving together.

> So I prophesied as He commanded me, and breath came into them, and they lived, and stood upon their feet, an exceedingly great army (Ezekiel 37:10).

• Corporate prayer is the power of agreement at its best.

> Again I say to you that if two of you agree on earth concerning anything that they ask, it will be done for them by My Father in heaven. For where two or three are gathered together in My name, I am there in the midst of them. (Matthew 18:19-20).

• Corporate prayer provides the power needed to bind the strong man.

> Assuredly, I say to you, whatever you bind on earth will be bound in heaven, and whatever you loose on earth will be loosed in heaven (Matthew 18:18).

• Corporate prayer can remove obstacles that stand in the way of spiritual advancement.

> Then it shall come to pass, when they make a long blast with the ram's horn, and when you hear the sound of the trumpet, that all the people

shall shout with a great shout; then the wall of the city will fall down flat. And the people shall go up every man straight before him (Joshua 6:5).

• Corporate prayer recognizes the spiritual principle of unity, activating that principle, and receiving benefits of corporate unity.

Behold, how good and how pleasant it is For brethren to dwell together in unity! It is like the precious oil upon the head, running down on the beard, the beard of Aaron, running down on the edge of his garments. It is like the dew of Hermon, Descending upon the mountains of Zion; for there the Lord commanded the blessing—life forevermore (Psalm 133).

• Corporate prayer may be used when some one in the local church is in great trial or need.

So, when he had considered this, he came to the house of Mary, the mother of John whose surname was Mark, where many were gathered together praying (Acts 12:12).

• Corporate prayer is a powerful expression of spiritual preparation as we enter into the corporate worship service.

Who may ascend into the hill of the Lord? Or who may stand in His holy place? He who has clean hands and a pure heart, who has not lifted up his soul to an idol, Nor sworn deceitfully. He shall receive blessing from the Lord, And righteousness from the God of his salvation (Psalm 24:3-5).

. . . .

Pre-service prayer will help the church enter God's presence with clean hands and a pure heart.

. . . .

Therefore, brethren, having boldness to enter the Holiest by the blood of Jesus, by a new and living way which He consecrated for us, through the veil, that is, His flesh, And having a High Priest over the house of God, let us draw near with a true heart in full assurance of faith, having our hearts sprinkled from an evil conscience and our bodies washed with pure water. Let us hold fast the confession of our hope without wavering, for He who promised is faithful (Hebrew 10:19-23).

Draw near to God and He will draw near to you. Cleanse your hands, you sinners; and purify your hearts, you double-minded (James 4:8).

The pre-service prayer time is especially suited to fulfill the need of people preparing to enter worship and hear the preached Word. Pre-service prayer helps the church enter into God's presence with clean hands and a pure heart.

The pre-service prayer time helps the church attune spiritual ears to hear the Word of God. People come to church with busy minds, filled with thoughts that are not always God pleasing, holy or edifying.

People need time to wash up before sitting down at His banqueting table.

• Corporate prayer should honor Christ as King, exalting His throne and His name with a spirit of gratefulness, and thanking him for His answers and His sovereignty.

> Therefore I exhort first of all that supplications, prayers, intercessions, and giving of thanks be made for all men (I Timothy 2:1).

• Corporate prayer prepares the atmosphere so that the Holy Spirit may move in power with an atmosphere of expectancy.

> And fixing his eyes on him, with John, Peter said, "Look at us." So he gave them his attention, expecting to receive something from them. Then Peter said, "Silver and gold I do not have, but what I do have I give you: In the name of Jesus Christ of Nazareth, rise up and walk" (Acts 3:4-6).

As the saying goes, sunshine flows to opened eyes. The church must cultivate a receiving frame of spirit and mind--a right attitude toward the gifts and the power of God. When a thirsty man comes to the fountain he holds his cup right side up.

• Corporate prayer can cultivate passion and faith for the harvest to be reaped.

> Fear not, for I am with you; I will bring your descendants from the east, and gather you from

the west; I will say to the north, 'Give them up!'
And to the south, 'Do not keep them back!' Bring
My sons from afar, and My daughters from the
ends of the earth--everyone who is called by My
name, whom I have created for My glory; I have
formed him, yes, I have made him" (Isaiah
43:5-7).

Then He said to His disciples, "The harvest truly
is plentiful, but the laborers are few. "Therefore
pray the Lord of the harvest to send out laborers
into His harvest" (Matthew 9:37-38).

John Geddie, the father of Presbyterian missions
in the South Seas, successfully reaped the harvest. The
inscription the islanders put in his church read, "When
he landed in 1848 there were no Christians. When he
left in 1872 there were no heathens."

If the church would only awaken to the responsibility of intercession, we would evangelize the world
in a short time. It is not God's plan that the world be
merely evangelized. Ultimately it should be evangelized in every generation.

Joel 2:1-9 is a call to corporate prayer. Let us
take heed.

- Blow the trumpet in Zion

- Sanctify a feast

- Call a solemn assembly

- Gather the people

- Sanctify the congregation

- Assemble the elders

- Gather the children

- Let the priests, the ministers of the Lord, weep

- Let them say "Spare thy people O Lord."

. . . .

Don't allow spiritual things to become commonplace.

. . . .

As praying worshippers let us enter each worship service with reverence and awe. God is greatly to be feared in the assembly of the saints. We must never take spiritual things for granted so that they become commonplace to us. Establishing a fervent Holy-Spirit-powered, pre-service prayer time will aid believers in the pursuit of spiritual preparation.

If prayer is esteemed highly by the Set Man and leadership, the congregation will follow. The Set Man should make a covenant with God concerning prayer like King Asa did in the Old Testament. King Asa received a wonderful, yet fearful prophetic word in II Chronicles 15:1-7. The prophetic word promised:

- The Lord will be with you if you are with Him.

- The Lord will let you find Him, if you are willing to seek Him.

- The Lord will forsake you if you forsake Him.

- The Lord will reward you if you seek Him.

II Chronicles 15:12 identifies the attitude every Set Man and every member of the leadership team should seek to establish.

> Then they entered into a covenant to seek the Lord God of their fathers with all their heart and with all their soul (II Chronicles 15:12).

> But from there you will seek the Lord your God, and you will find Him if you seek Him with all your heart and with all your soul. When you are in distress, and all these things come upon you in the latter days, when you turn to the Lord your God and obey His voice (for the Lord your God is a merciful God), He will not forsake you nor destroy you, nor forget the covenant of your fathers which He swore to them (Deuteronomy 4:29-31).

> Glory in His holy name; let the hearts of those rejoice who seek the Lord! Seek the Lord and His strength; seek His face evermore! (II Chronicles 16:10-11).

> Now set your heart and your soul to seek the Lord your God. Therefore arise and build the sanctuary of the Lord God, to bring the ark of the covenant of the Lord and the holy articles of God into the house that is to be built for the name of the Lord (I Chronicles 22:19).

> If My people who are called by My name will humble themselves, and pray and seek My face,

and turn from their wicked ways, then I will hear from heaven, and will forgive their sin and heal their land (II Chronicles 7:14).

God's people must be willing to commit themselves to a covenant of seeking the face of the Lord--a commitment made by an oath. Give us leaders like King Asa who will call the church to a prayer covenant during these momentous times.

CHAPTER EIGHTEEN

THE SET MAN AND HIS DREAMS

Highlights

- God desires to help us develop our full potential and realize our purpose in life.

- A Set Man with a powerful vision or dream will energize everyone around him.

- The more the Set Man feeds on the Word of God the more focused he will become.

- Surround yourself with wholesome relationships that are in unity with your dream.

- The Set Man must be a dreamer, intense and focused.

Hope deferred makes the heart sick,
but when dreams come true at last there is life and joy.
—Proverbs 13:12 LB

The future belongs to those who have dreams. All great men and women have been motivated by their God-given dreams. People who have a plan and the faith to live out their dreams truly live a life of excitement and fulfillment. God desires to help us develop our full potential and bring into reality our purpose in life. He has a definite life plan for every person, girding them visibly or invisibly for some exact task. That task will be the true significance and glory of the life which has accomplished it.

> Live life, then, with a due sense of responsibility, not as men who do not know the meaning of life but as those who do. Make the best use of your time, despite all the evils of these days (Ephesians 5:15-16 PHILLIPS).

> Look carefully then how you walk! Live purposefully and worthily and accurately, not as the unwise and witless, but as wise--sensible, intelligent people; making the very most of the time-- buying up each opportunity--because the days are evil (Ephesians 5:15-16 AMPLIFIED).

John Killinger tells the story of hearing W. Clement Stone, the Chicago financier and philanthropist reply to the question, "How have you done so much in your lifetime?" Stone explained, "I have dreamed. I have turned my mind loose to imagine what I wanted to do. Then I have gone to bed and thought about my dreams. In the night I have dreamed about them. And when I have risen in the morning I have seen the way to get to my dreams. While other people were saying, 'You can't do that; it isn't possible.' I was well on my way to achieving what I wanted."

. . . .

The Set Man with a powerful vision will energize everyone around him.

. . . .

This is the awesome power of having a dream--a burning desire deep within that creates energy. This is the energy propelling the Set Man into action.

A Set Man with a powerful vision or dream will energize everyone around him. What would you do with your life or attempt to do if you knew it was impossible to fail?

. . . .

A vision or dream deserves and demands focus.

. . . .

God begins every potential miracle in your life with a faith picture born of the Holy Spirit. This invisible idea, this invisible vision, will eventually give birth to a visible, tangible fulfillment.

Our dreams and visions begin as undeveloped pictures deep within our hearts and minds--things we see God wants to do in the future. The more the Set Man, feeds on the Word of God with understanding, the more focused he becomes. The purpose of God becomes more and more clear as he articulates the biblical vision.

Vision creates a bright future, increases our motivation level, and supplies a mighty stimulus to work hard for fulfillment. Vision will separate you to your destiny. It seals destiny. As Socrates said, "We have a better chance of hitting the target if we can see it."

To dream is to:

• Anticipate what is coming to pass and contemplate it with pleasure.

• Have a fond hope or aspiration for the future.

• Face obstacles with the determination of a winner.

• Set specific goals by which to mark achievement.

• Look beyond what is to bring about what should be.

Where there is no vision, the people perish: but he that keepeth the law, happy is he (Proverbs 29:18).

Every Set Man needs to become a Joseph in the kingdom of God. Joseph was a man of strength and clear purpose. He was a man who had a clear destiny. Joseph is a prophetic picture of all who dream God's dreams and then pay the price to make them reality. (See Genesis 37-50; Psalm 105:17)

> Now Joseph dreamed a dream, and he told it to his brothers; and they hated him even more (Genesis 37:5).

> Then he dreamed still another dream and told it to his brothers, and said, "Look, I have dreamed another dream. And this time, the sun, the moon, and the eleven stars bowed down to me" (Genesis 37:9).

> Joseph's dreams were God-given and his future was God-governed. Vision and dreams many times focus only on the end result, the advancement promised. The test, pain, trials, sorrow, hardships, delays and disappointments are usually not in the dream. As the saying goes, "Happy are those who dream dreams and are ready to pay the price to make them come true."

. . . .

A specific target will allow the team to pull all their strength together toward one unified vision.

. . . .

A dream is a mission statement in life, a determined goal that is God inspired, resulting in kingdom extension and kingdom fruitfulness.

Call to Me, and I will answer you, and show you great and mighty things, which you do not know (Jeremiah 33:3).

But there is a spirit in man, and the breath of the Almighty gives him understanding (Job 32:8).

Delight yourself also in the Lord, And He shall give you the desires of your heart (Psalm 37:4).

The Lord will inspire the heart of the Set Man with a vision for God's purpose. This vision or dream deserves and demands focus, keeping your eye on your goal. You will never accomplish your vision without a strong desire. Visualization will fuel the fire of your God-birthed vision.

Desire is the starting place of achievement. (See Hebrews 12:2; Matthew 6:22; Psalm 101:3). As you move toward the vision God gives you, surround yourself with wholesome relationships that are in unity with your dream. You can lose motivation for your dream by being around faithless, small-minded, world-centered people (Proverbs 13:20). Dare to reach for the companionship of great thinkers.

Invest in good books, absorb their spirit and the victorious attitudes that have driven them to success. *Transforming Leadership* by Leighton Ford, and *Renewing Our Ministry* by David McKenn are life-shaping books.

Read autobiographies of great men and women who accomplished their dreams. Get inspired by their sacrificial living, their never- give-up attitude. Absorb, absorb, absorb!

Read books that stretch your thinking capacity like *The Closing of the American Mind* by Bloom. Another book from the secular world which will help shape your thinking as a visionary is *The Man Who Discovered Quality* by Anvaea Gabor. This is a book about W. Edward Deming, the American who revolutionized product excellence in Japan over twenty years ago, and came back to an obviously failing American auto industry.

. . . .

Most people plan more for a one week vacation than they do for their life journey.

. . . .

The Set Man must be a dreamer, a man of rare gifting for intensity and focus. The Set Man must focus his entire life on the dream. A specific target, a specific faith goal will allow team members to pull all their strength together toward a unified vision.

The dream of the Set Man must become the dominant passion in his life, filling up every available space within him, crowding out every distraction and every adversity.

A person will always move in the direction of his most dominant thought. Use your imagination, that invisible machine inside your mind which has the power to create God-given vision, pictures of destiny in technicolor. Great achievers learn to replay memories of their past triumphs and preplay pictures of their desired successes.

The Set Man must not only dream great dreams, but make plans to bring them to pass.

For a dream comes through the multitude of much business and painful effort (Ecclesiastes 5:3).

Any enterprise is built by wise planning, becomes strong through common sense, and profits wonderfully by keeping abreast of the facts (Proverbs 24:3 LB).

Create blueprints for the dream God has given you. Many leaders have great dreams, but no plans to bring them to reality. Most people plan more for a one week vacation than they do for their life journey!

Commit your works to the Lord, and you plans will be established (Proverbs 16:3).

God loves a planner. God respects people who think enough of their dreams to create plans for their attainment. Noah had a plan for the ark. Moses had a plan for the tabernacle.

. . . .

D̲on't give up in the midst of discouragement or severe testing.

. . . .

The Set Man is called to be an achiever. Rise up today and begin to dream great dreams with God. D.L. Moody gave His sons some great advice upon his death bed. He said, "If God be your partner, make your plans big!" Let us not give in to mediocrity. Let us not give up in the midst of discouragement or severe testing. Let us take heed to Long-fellow's words. "Great is the art of beginning, but greater the art of finishing." We are called to finish the vision totally. Let us fix our eyes on the Apostle Paul, the great visionary as he finished his course.

Paul finished without shipwrecking. He lived his dream. He died with satisfaction. He could triumphantly say, "I did my best! I chose the best! I served the best!" Let all leaders become like Paul in his passion and perseverance in living out his dream.

- Paul poured his life out like a drink offering.

  For I am already being poured out as a drink offering, and the time of my departure is at hand (II Timothy 4:6).

- Paul successfully triumphed over obstacles in his race.

  I have fought the good fight, I have finished the race, I have kept the faith (II Timothy 4:7).

- Paul kept the faith in the midst of quitters.

  For Demas has forsaken me, having loved this present world, and has departed for Thessalonica--Crescens for Galatia, Titus for Dalmatia (II Timothy 4:10).

- Paul kept his eyes on the true Judge Who sees all things, past, present, and future.

  Finally, there is laid up for me the crown of righteousness, which the Lord, the righteous Judge, will give to me on that day, and not to me only but also to all who have loved His appearing (II Timothy 4:8).

• Paul cultivated a forgiving spirit. He didn't blame others for his trials.

At my first defense no one stood with me, but all forsook me. May it not be charged against them (II Timothy 4:16).

• Paul's secret of strength was his conscious awareness that God always stood with him. He was never alone!

But the Lord stood with me and strengthened me, so that the message might be preached fully through me, and that all the Gentiles might hear. And I was delivered out of the mouth of the lion. And the Lord will deliver me from every evil work and preserve me for His heavenly kingdom. To Him be glory forever and ever. Amen! (II Timothy 4;17-18).

Success is to be measured not so much by the position one has reached in life, as the obstacles which he has overcome while trying to succeed.
                                    --Booker T. Washington

APPENDIX

THE HIGH CALLING

If God has called you to be really like Jesus in all your spirit, He will draw you into a life of crucifixion and humility, and put on you such demands of obedience that He will not allow you to follow other Christians, and in many ways He will seem to let other good people do things which He will not let you do.

Other Christians and ministers who seem very religious and useful may push themselves, pull wires, and work schemes to carry out their plans, but you cannot do it; and if you attempt it, you will meet with such failure and rebuke from the Lord as to make you sorely penitent.

Others can brag on themselves, on their work, on their success, on their writings, but the Holy Spirit will not allow you to do any such thing, and if you begin it, He will lead you into some deep mortification that will make you despise yourself and all your good works.

Others will be allowed to succeed in making great sums of money, or having a legacy left to them or in having luxuries, but God may supply you daily, because He wants you to have something far better than gold, and that is a helpless dependence on Him, that He may have the privilege of providing your need day by day out of the unseen treasury.

God will let others be great, but keep you small. He will let others do a work for Him, and get the credit for it, but He will make you work and toil on without knowing how much you are doing; and then to make your work still more precious He will let others get the credit for the work which you have done, and this will make your reward ten times greater when Jesus comes.

The Holy Spirit will put a strict watch on you, with a jealous love, and will rebuke you for little words and feelings or for wasting your time, which other Christians never seem distressed over. So make up your mind that God is an infinite Sovereign, and He has a right to do as He pleases with His own, and He will not explain to you a thousand things which may puzzle your reason in His dealings with you.

God will take you at your word; and if you absolutely sell yourself to be His slave, He will wrap you up in a jealous love, and let other people say and do many things that you cannot do or say. Settle it forever that you are to deal directly with the Holy Spirit, and that He is to have the privilege of tying your tongue, or chaining your hand, or closing your eyes, in ways that others are not dealt with.

Now when you are so possessed with the living God, that you are in your secret heart pleased and delighted over this peculiar personal, private, jealous guardianship and management of the Holy Spirit over your life, you will have found the vestibule of heaven.

--Author Unknown

INDEX

NOTES

1. Frank Damazio, *The Making of a Leader*. (Portland: Bible Temple Publishing, 1988)

2. Howard Snyder, *The Problem With Wineskins*. (Illinois: Inter-varsity Press, 1975).

3. Bill Hull, *The Disciple Making Pastor*. (Old Tappan: Fleming H. Revell, 1988).

4. Gene Edwards, *The Tale of Three Kings*. (Auburn: Christian Books).

5. Thomas Gillespie, *The Laity in Biblical Perspective*.

6. George Barna, *The Frog in the Kettle; The User Friendly Church*. (Ventura: Regal Books, 1990, 1991).

7. Jack Hayford, *Prayer-Invading the Impossible*. (Plainfield: Logos International, 1977).

8. Yongi Cho, *Prayer-Key to Revival*. (Waco: Word Books, 1984).

Note

The *California Inventory Test* referred to on page 131, paragraph 2 can be found at:

Consulting Psychological Press
3803 E Bayshore Road
Palo Alto, CA 94303

Phone: (415) 969-8901
Fax: (415) 969-8606

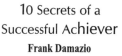

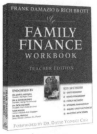